KAPLAN McLAUGHLIN DIAZ

Rockport Publishers
Gloucester, Massachusetts
Distributed by North Light Books
Cincinnati, Ohio

KAPLAN McLAUGHLIN DIAZ

PLACEMAKING:

INNOVATION AND INDIVIDUALITY

Richard Rapaport

First published in the United States of America by:
Rockport Publishers, Inc.
33 Commercial Street
Gloucester, Massachusetts 01930-5089
Telephone: (978) 282-9590
Fax: (978) 283-2742

ISBN 1-56496-236-9

10 9 8 7 6 5 4 3 2 1

Printed in China

Design and composition:
Group C Inc / New Haven/Boston
Brad Collins, Christopher Kirby, Fredric Schaub, Amanda Turn, Catharine Weese, Elizabeth Zimmerman
Brad Collins, Christopher Kirby, Fredric Schaub,
Amanda Turn, Catharine Weese, Elizabeth Zimmerman

Text for this book was set in Adobe Caslon 540.

Front cover: Oakland Federal Building
    Photograph © Richard Barnes
Back cover, top: Two Rodeo Drive
    Photograph © Paul Bielenberg
Back cover, bottom: UCSD Medical Center
    Photograph © David Hewitt/Anne Garrison
Front flap: K. K. Nakazato Corporate Headquarters
    Photograph © Kokyu Miwa Photo Laboratory
Back flap: Marin General Hospital
    Photograph © Tom Rider
Title page: Price Center
    Photograph © Nick Merrick, Hedrich Blessing

The work of Kaplan McLaughlin Diaz (KMD) spans more than three decades and represents an unprecedented range of project type and location. To create this significant body of work required the intelligence, creativity and dedication of numerous people. Through the years KMD has been viewed as a testing ground for new ideas, a school for bright young architects, an incubator for research topics, and a place where people are encouraged to question accepted paradigms. The result of this energy, creativity and questioning is an architecture of diversity, creative and innovative, but difficult to categorize, describe or encapsulate in a book.

This book was a labor not just of love, but persistence, energy and vision. The fact that it comes close to illustrating the heart and soul of our firm is the result of an intense effort by a relatively small group of people, significant for both their individual and cumulative contributions to KMD.

Herb McLaughlin was the prompter of ideas for the book. His commitment to innovative thinking carries over from KMD's architecture to the ideas presented in this volume. As a guide, creative force, critic and coach his insight and intellect have motivated the firm to seek the unique solution to design and planning challenges. Richard Rappaport handled the job of writer with intelligence and understanding, and completed the daunting task of transforming visual ideas into literary insights. Brad Collins and the staff at Group C honed and sharpened the design of the book, using design skills and a dispassionate eye to create a persuasive document that also reveals a lively story. Gavin Bardes, new to KMD, handled the almost thankless task of managing this task with wit and wisdom well beyond his years. And Rockport Press gave berth to our idiosyncrasies while helping maintain a working schedule. Without all these efforts, "Individualism and Innovation" would not exist.

Most important, without the creativity, ingenuity and shear sweat of a generation of KMD'ers there would be no story to tell in the first place. The significant design insights of Herb McLaughlin, the depth of knowledge illustrated by the work of Jim Diaz, and the intelligent questioning and contributions of dozens of key designers, planners, thinkers and dreamers have extended the reach and depth of our practice. This firm is an intellectually heady environment; always questioning, never stagnant, but it is never dull and never takes a safe path. This book acknowledges the people who created the culture, and the body of work this environment has produced.

Board of Directors

Oakland, California, the very same Oakland about which Jazz Age writer Gertude Stein complained "there is no there there," looms in the distance, a half-dozen miles across the bay from San Francisco. The view is part of the vivid panorama southeast from the fourth floor of the spare, converted foot-of-Telegraph-Hill coffee warehouse that is the headquarters of Kaplan McLaughlin Diaz.

Encompassed in that scene of the Bay Bridge and beyond are the twin eighteen-story towers of the Oakland Federal Building. Completed in 1993, the KMD-designed Federal Building has become the figurative gateway to a revitalized Oakland downtown. But if those towers symbolize the broad strokes of a city's rebirth, the Federal Building's plazas, gardens, and glowing central rotunda stand as something less lofty, more intimate, and possibly more important. Already a much-used, well-loved public space for Oaklanders to gather, the Federal Building is a place that in part puts modern-day lie to Ms. Stein's wonderfully intemperate bon mot.

The notion that the Oakland Federal Building has put the "there there" may be slightly hyperbolic. But the concept of the creation of an important place through the KMD-conceived concept of civic "placemaking" is not. Rather, "sense of place" and "placemaking" are powerful chords running through the architecture of KMD. Placemaking, as practiced by the firm, might be defined as the ability to discover in the intelligent partitioning of physical space, an exciting, yet comfortable, public place capable of promoting a sense of unity, of well-being, and of community.

Over the last four decades, KMD's practice has covered a uniquely diverse range of building types: retail, health care, academic, hotel, government, offices, housing, historic preservation and renovation. KMD designs have been built in a wide variety of geographic areas including the U.S., Japan, Mexico, Malaysia, China, and France, supported by offices in cities all over the globe.

That there is a broad diversity in KMD's work is unquestionable. Indeed, the notion that creative and highly individual solutions must be found that are unique to a client, to a program and/or a location, is central to KMD's ethos as an architectural firm. Along the way, this focus on the discovery of individual, creative and humane solutions has produced imaginative and important contributions to the palette of late-twentieth-century architecture. There is a long list of KMD architectural discoveries that might go under chapter headings such as "The Movie Theater as Marquee," "Megafloors in Medical Office Buildings," "Multiple Ground Floors for Higher Profit Retail," "The Urban Entertainment Center—Celebratory Spaces for Fun and Profit," and so on. More important, from the KMD perspective, these innovations—and the process that created them—have helped increase the number of buildings around the planet that contribute to a sense of human scale and of place.

Because if there is a theme running through all of KMD's work, it is that of placemaking.

Placemaking suggests that to be successful a project needs to cast its own spell on its user and community. Placemaking is both a sensitivity to place and the creation of uniquely useable space. Placemaking realizes in the buildings and, equally important, in the spaces defined by the buildings, a shared sense of community, a connection with the essence of one's culture in an entertaining and joyful way. This has contributed to the success of such KMD projects as San Francisco's Galaxy Theater; the University of San Diego's Price Center; Two Rodeo Drive in Beverly Hills; International Market Square in Minneapolis; the Morning Park Chikaramachi Retirement Community in Nagoya, Japan; Brigham & Women's Hospital in Boston, and others.

OAKLAND FEDERAL BUILDING

Placemaking is not a matter of happenstance. To be effective, placemaking requires that a number of serious considerations be taken into account from a project's initial conception. These include such things as recognizing the architectural impact on users, promoting human interaction, developing a context that responds to the scale of the surrounding environment, and connecting with roots often traceable to indigenous design. Placemaking also requires an understanding and love of the history of the built world.

A powerful, historical sense of place is so integral to the life of so many ancient communities that no single individual or group can claim credit for the strong social appeal of squares, cloisters, or piazzas that still define the life of cities like London, Paris, Rome, and Venice. Creating these types of celebrated and, as KMD renders them, "celebratory" places in today's building environment demands a deep understanding of the dynamics of place, of sensitive planning, and of innovative design on a human scale.

Indeed, the failure of so many plazas and atria built over the last thirty-five years to create such a sense of community in an urban context has come close to giving public space a bad name in the design community and, more importantly, in the popular perception. Lifeless windswept plazas, often dropped in front of high-rises for the purpose of gaining zoning variances that will allow taller, often less appropriate buildings and more rentable square footage, or vast atria displaying little awareness of human scale, have little to do with creating a sense of community, intimacy, or celebration— the irreducible minimums of placemaking.

KMD's research, a critical part of its process of architectural discovery, and the success of many of its projects strongly suggest that such failures are not so much a lack of need or interest in these spaces as the consequence of bad design judgment and poor execution.

To discover and analyze the root elements of placemaking, KMD conducted what has become a landmark study published under the title *Urban Agoras*. Prompted by the highly pragmatic concern of how best to address large public spaces in major renovation and planning projects, the findings and observations still continue to guide KMD's design hand. As the name of the study indicates, it leads back to the concept of the "Agora," the public market in ancient Greece where the life of the polity was played out with such import for the development of western civilization. Part seat of government, part center of commerce, part showcase for arts and crafts, the Agora proves a worthwhile model for contemporary urban design.

At its heart, the study suggested, the Agora is a form committed to the elemental human need to be at the center of things. And the "architecture," if it could even be called that, that supported the success of the Agora was irregular in nature, human in scale, and composed of a number of complimentary elements, such as water features, landscaping, and humanly scaled "off-stage" corners and niches that could be both balance against and antidote to the large open spaces.

Architecturally, the placemaking model of the Agora, and the corresponding attempt to create what the firm calls celebratory space, has found meaning in almost every type of KMD project—civic centers, hospitals, housing, retail facilities, academic structures, university campuses, and office complexes. From the glowing lobby at San Francisco's Galaxy Theater to the crowded piazza at UC San Diego's Price Center, to the spare, landscaped central courtyard at Morning Park Chikaramachi

MORNING PARK CHIKARAMACHI
RETIREMENT COMMUNITY

ONE COLORADO

PANAMBI

Retirement Community in Nagoya, to the grassy enclosed cloister in the Business Administration and Education Building at Cal Poly, San Luis Obispo; the spirit of the Agora has transformed built space into well-liked, humanly scaled and highly livable places.

In these projects and others, the art of placemaking involves the simultaneous creation of congregating places with intimate subspaces that help draw in those people who are initially intimidated by large, open space. Another fundamental characteristic of placemaking involves enticing users with attractive interior environments that appear to flow directly from their carefully landscaped exterior surroundings. When properly handled, this can result in a highly charged, interactive architecture that invites participation and engages users rather than shutting them out.

Placemaking is an architectural approach leading to the creation of a genuine sense of place that both draws people in and entertains them while they are there. This sense of invitation is enhanced by incorporating features such as well-defined entry points, campaniles or landmark towers, scaling elements like trellises and plantings, and textured materials that create a feeling of substance. The goal is to introduce a measure of the intimacy, scale, and comfort that large-scale urban development has largely neglected in the contemporary environment. And to KMD the qualities of the space are as important as the architecture that surrounds it.

In retail applications such as One Colorado Boulevard in Pasadena and the Price Center at UC San Diego, the creation of a piazza where one did not exist before has produced phenomenal financial returns and added a heightened level of energy and excitement to the surrounding area. People flock to these and other KMD examples of celebratory retail placemaking, in no small part because the architecture itself adds so much delight to the overall ambience and experience.

Placemaking, as interpreted by KMD, owes as much to the classic academic cloister as it does to the highly activated town square. In institutional projects, such as those for Brigham & Women's Hospital, UC San Diego's Price Center and Cal Poly, San Luis Obispo, creative placemaking helps facilities gain a sense of identity, promotes bonding between institution and individual, and creates an authentic sense of human scale and community where little existed before.

In planning and civic projects, such as the Oakland Federal Building; International Design Center, Nagoya, Japan; the Panambi Development in São Paulo, Brazil; and the New Shanghai International Plaza in Shanghai, China; well-designed public spaces are planned for high levels of public use and have contributed to the reweaving of often-dissociated central civic areas.

Particularly in KMD's Asian projects, highly activated retail plazas bring a much needed sense of community to the often-crowded streets that surround the locations. KMD has found that the ideals of placemaking are highly exportable and citizens of cities such as Shanghai, Nagoya, and Hiroshima that lacked the amenities of public celebratory space, welcome placemaking projects enthusiastically.

The notion of architectural placemaking finds an important corollary in KMD's sense of its own place as a design organization. Since the firm's founding, KMD has always striven to be a place that is at once intimate, celebratory, and communal.

An example of this is the weekly Design Review which throughout KMD's existence has contributed key ideas to important projects. Design Reviews discourage tunnel vision and act as a purgative for prima donna architecture. They have also been the catalyst for young associates with a particular flash of insight or interest to be drafted into career-enhancing projects.

Reflecting KMD's reputation for provocative thought and design, the review is often tumultuous; participants are invited to probe, test, and find better solutions to the design problems. The result is an exuberant and often sharp-edged architectural conversation, egged on by Herb McLaughlin, design principal, acting as iconoclastic ringmaster.

Design Reviews are egalitarian; partners and associates, architectural and nonarchitectural employees alike are encouraged to contribute ideas and criticism. There is one sacred rule for Design Reviews: any drawing or plan tacked to the wall will be marked up, commented upon, and turned inside out.

Celebratory activities at the firm take the form of regular free-form, extracurricular diversions including design roundtables, debates with entertaining notions such as "Classicism is Not a Style" (KMD decided it was not).

There is the yearly, tongue-firmly-in-cheek "Seven Days in May" festival, a competition for solutions to such nonrevenue–producing projects as the Monument to the Unknown Yuppie, Regionalism as Applied to a HotDog Stand, a Portable Papal Podium, a San Francisco Street Toilet, etc. Laurels come in the form of prizes such as a pass to a local shooting range for "Most On-Target Scheme." Regular screenings of architecturally related movies are held, including of course the Cary Grant classic, *Mr. Blanding Builds His Dream House*. KMD has also produced well-received books, such as the *Designer's Guide to Good Eats*, a spicy architect's view of Bay Area restaurants, and *Hidden L.A.*, a Northern Californian look at the Southland, produced in conjunction with the San Francisco Museum of Modern Art.

The effect of these activities, which might initially seem like frivolity, is anything but frivolous. It has helped create a highly desirable place to work, an élan that is a KMD hallmark, and several decades' worth of recognized, award-winning, and exceptionally well-placed projects.

And KMD's own well-grounded sense of place in the architectural universe is also evident in the urge to collaborate. So comfortable is KMD working with other architectural firms that it promotes collaboration on projects more than two hours by air from a KMD office. KMD has worked successfully with firms in Latin America, Europe, and Asia; receiving and transmitting insights, information and skills.

In the end, however, KMD's design philosophy is both highly singular and easily definable. The firm's most basic convictions are grounded in the fundamental belief that great architecture is less a matter of style than of discovery—of finding ways to connect function, need, context, and most importantly, as we shall see, to develop a unique sense of place.

NADYA PARK INTERNATIONAL DESIGN CENTER

SHANGHAI INTERNATIONAL PLAZA

11

PRICE CENTER
UNIVERSITY OF CALIFORNIA, SAN DIEGO

Stroll the gently curving Via Rodeo thoroughfare that is the centerpiece of Two Rodeo Drive in Beverly Hills. Contemplate the multiform panorama of UC San Diego's Price Center from the set-back "Nerd's Walk" parapet. Or happily browse the many and varied niches, viewpoints, and recesses inside the atrium of the International Market Square in Minneapolis. The heart of each of these experiences, and a defining trademark of KMD design, is the element of discovery. It is the verity that the architecture is not revealed in a single glance, but rather as an unfolding exploration of the emotion of design that draws participants along to see for themselves what new revelation might be waiting around the next corner.

Not coincidentally, there is a similar, defining tenet in the evolution of KMD itself. It is the conviction that the life of the firm has, at its best, been a voyage of discovery, a romantic exploration born of an eagerness to find something new and challenging in every commission. The very diversity of the practice over the years argues for this notion of architectural exploration, as does the willingness to undertake a wide range of firm-funded research.

KMD's dedication to research is intense and goes well beyond the scope of typical design industry concerns. Indeed, much of KMD's research is unconnected to any project at all and is instead undertaken to discover answers to larger concerns of design philosophy.

When a project is involved, research often means an intensive discussion with clients, owners, and users prior to a project's planning. The objective is to provoke a discussion of a particular set of architectural needs, as well as an understanding of the emotional underpinnings of a client's sense of place and individuality. Whatever its point of departure, research as undertaken by KMD is a simple, unique and profoundly powerful architectural tool of discovery.

The KMD research cycle often begins with an intensive, investigative effort at a project's inception, an effort meant to define underlying issues and concerns. And research applies both to anticipated as well as completed projects, from which many valuable lessons can be learned.

INTERNATIONAL MARKET SQUARE

If research is the front door to a project, postoccupancy reviews are its rear exits. At the conclusion of a design project, at the point when most firms are converting plans to microfilm, KMD is sending an evaluation team in to study the finished project. The team normally includes an outside architect, end-users, and an environmental psychologist or sociologist. These often brutally frank postoccupancy reviews of a number of KMD projects have helped increase KMD's knowledge base, design expertise, and methodology.

The combination of predesign research and postoccupancy review has been a catalyst for the firm's evolution and a way to apply lessons learned in one project type to what may seem superficially to be totally unrelated territory. Thus, solutions for retirement facilities have illuminated the way to better student unions, student unions have led to more valuable retail spaces, and more valuable retail space has led to more humane retirement and mental health facilities.

In 1963 the Federal Mental Health Act demanded fundamental changes in the psychiatric treatment of mentally ill patients. In effect, the act deinstitutionalized thousands and placed them back in their communities as outpatients.

Thus, the community mental health center emerged as the place for short-term acute intervention rather than long-term care and housing. In response to this sea change in health care, KMD founders Herb McLaughlin and Ellis Kaplan co-authored, with two practicing psychiatrists, a study titled "Planning, Programming and Designing the Community Mental Health Center." The study became a landmark for the planning of a totally new type of facility. It also contained the basic tenets of inquiry and innovation that fostered numerous planning and design discoveries and breakthroughs over the firm's thirty-plus years.

BRIGHAM & WOMEN'S HOSPITAL

Subsequent KMD hospital studies have taken an even broader, groundbreaking look at the fundamental integration of design into the curative process. KMD research into patterns of obsolescence in hospitals, for example, elaborated new ways of designing health facilities to extend their useful lives. It discovered ways to make remodeling, when it became necessary, a far less disruptive process. A study titled "Prototypes for Design of Hospitals" established protocols for the kind of asset management that has gained currency throughout the American design community in recent years.

This particular inquiry analyzed changes in six hospitals over a twenty-year period. Based on these findings, KMD developed a planning approach that centered around the concept of looking at the prototype of "hospital as village." This simple, yet innovative, concept was responsible for fundamentally revising the process of healthcare facility design decision making. It suggested, among other things, that while it might previously have been acceptable to force uncomplimentary medical elements into tightly defined structures, the village concept allowed various service units to grow and change over time by organizing them along a central horizontal spine or, as termed by KMD—and executed at facilities such as Brigham & Women's Hospital in Boston—"Medical Main Street."

Historically KMD has allocated approximately 2 percent of its yearly budget to research and pro bono projects. "Inquiries," as these explorations are referred to in the firm, are generally initiated by challenges presented by particular clients and projects.

WASHINGTON/MONTGOMERY TOWER

Nonmedical-related firm research has focused on areas such as the unique housing needs of the elderly, the creation of active public spaces on the university campus, the development of an exciting environment in retail centers, and the export of the celebratory piazza to Asia.

Ground-breaking, non-health care-related studies include reuse plan for Denver's Stapleton Airport, the "Tall Buildings/Tight Streets" study to determine the most useful design features for high-rise buildings on urban alleys, and a KMD/Ford Foundation collaboration into the efficiency of school classroom sizes. This study determined what the most useful and economical educational modules might look like.

CENTRAL PLAZA

PROYECTO PEDREGAL

Two early research projects, a study into the "Manhattanization" of San Francisco and an inquiry into the development of urban celebratory space, addressed the important contextual needs of cities.

The first of these was undertaken in the late 1960s to look at a new generation of downtown development in San Francisco that involved the assemblage of megasites and the design of towering, bulky skyscrapers. Many feared that San Francisco would become as densely developed as Manhattan, thus losing the light and air quality and the spectacular views for which it was famous. KMD worked with local planning groups on a comprehensive study analyzing the appropriate scale for future development. The study provided a methodology for controlling the development of large-scale high-rises while providing a game plan for overall growth in the city. Many of its proposals were incorporated in San Francisco's landmark 1985 Downtown Development Plan. Perhaps KMD's most significant research project was its "Urban Agora" study, mentioned in the introduction. "Urban Agoras" was a multiyear look into the design of lively urban, civic spaces. The study determined that successful public spaces share characteristics in common, many of which could be incorporated into a diverse range of building types and applicable to both interior and exterior spaces alike.

The study also made the point that well-designed public spaces, including atria, plazas, parks, or shopping centers, could help make up for the loss of social and physical landmarks in modern society. These celebratory spaces could serve the unifying function that railroad stations, churches, and town halls had held in less alienated times. "Urban Agoras" concluded by suggesting that by incorporating celebratory and humanizing features into designs for large public spaces, modern urban spaces could also help fill the critical contemporary need for shared experiences, as well as create a critical emotional response in users.

At its most profound, KMD's ongoing commitment to discovery through research can be measured in this ability to facilitate emotion through design. Many of the most important discoveries over the years were the simplest, most emotional, and personal. In one of KMD's earliest projects, for example the Martin Luther King Square housing project in San Francisco, simple, but profound truths were uncovered simply by asking questions no one else thought to ask.

In the late 1940s and early '50s, it turned out, asbestos shingle salesmen blanketed the Afro-American community in San Francisco and then blanketed buildings with ugly, but durable asbestos siding. KMD research uncovered a popular distaste for shingles that extended into the '60s and '70s and even applied to redwood and cedar siding. Another approach was tried. The resulting design was a clean, modern approach to low-rise family housing, rather than being derivative of established San Francisco shingle style.

A similar discovery was made that there was a widely differing perception of the desirability of street access to housing depending on the age of the resident. While younger families wanted a direct link between their homes and the street, older residents found the street threatening. Instead of entrances on the street, they preferred housing that had interior entryways and guarded entrances. KMD was thus able to respond with a design containing both open "front stoop" entrances and shielded, interior courtyards.

KMD's self-funded research studies and postoccupancy reviews also equate with the firm's sense of public-spiritedness and the possibility, as elaborated in the "Urban Agoras" study, of creating an architecture that "gives back." Much of KMD's work is illuminated by the notion that the healing principle of integrated "village" life can be applied to different modern design dysfunctions. Even more importantly, this "healing design," if properly applied, can provide a remedy for some of the societal dysfunctionality heretofore only made more dire by alienating architecture.

The notion of giving back also lies behind the number of published opinion, magazine pieces and essays that come out of KMD on a regular basis. These are manifestations of both a high degree of concern about the life of modern design and a facility with the written word highly developed for the architectural profession. Perhaps most important, this public interchange is indicative of an overall sense of the emotional connection between design and living and the importance of seeing life and architecture as an evolving process of discovery.

CELEBRATING DESIGN
ON A HUMAN SCALE

Such a volume of KMD's work has been set in an urban context that it is natural for the firm to have developed strong fundamental principles regarding the nature of placemaking and the creation of celebratory, human-scaled space in the modern city. This same spirit animates the firm's work in campus settings both academic and corporate, which KMD recognizes as an important corollary to the urban experience. The firm has applied over three decades of discovery—gained through study, observation, and revisiting completed projects—to fine-tuning its approach to these urban and campus projects.

The resulting design philosophy builds upon context, respects the scale of the surrounding built environment and at the same time, is highly cognizant of the interaction between people and architecture. This, in turn, has led to a portfolio of innovative projects that, taken as a whole, illustrate the values of design practiced at a human scale.

Projects as diverse as college campuses, retail centers, hospitals, and government office buildings promote an active relationship between people, buildings, and activities that promote a vital, yet safe, urban street scene. In the KMD vision, both city and campus are anything but an isolated series of buildings. Rather, they are interactive and alive with rich context, defining contrasts and attention to human scale.

KMD's "human scale" design philosophy began taking shape with the firm's earliest commissions, such as the 1968 Martin Luther King Square housing development in San Francisco. The design for this project grew out of research and observation to assess the housing needs of lower income residents. KMD came to a series of conclusions: that a community thrives on commerce and social interaction, that there was a vital symbiosis between public and private space and that "popular" projects are universally profitable. And though the Martin Luther King project was purely housing, the insights gained lead to a series of innovative and profitable mixed-use and retail projects as well as a healthy export of related architecture to Asia.

MARTIN LUTHER KING SQUARE

KMD's commitment to research led to studies that focused on the introduction of new development into the urban context and the need for large-scale projects to take into account the importance of urban street life, a sense of scale, and the complexity of human interaction.

From early on, KMD recognized the benefits and vitality of mixed-use projects. Thus, the firm refused to accept the standard of high-rise office or residential towers built on top of platform plazas inaccessible from the street. Mixed-use projects such as Stevenson Place and the Washington/Montgomery Tower were designed specifically to embrace the street. These and other projects exemplified the ideal of architecture at a human scale by providing lively, interactive facades that reached out to passersby and, in some cases, brought the street, in the form of pedestrian walkways and ground floor cut-backs, inside the building.

OAKLAND FEDERAL BUILDING

This focus on interaction is well illustrated in the design of the Federal Building in Oakland, California. Though a government office tower, particularly one with court facilities at ground level, seldom develops as a well-loved local gathering place, this project has been singled out as one of the major reasons for the revitalization of adjacent portions of downtown Oakland. The reason is simple: A welcoming plaza is open to all, as is the building's large atrium/lobby. The overall project extends the basic block pattern of the area, while providing comfortable gathering spaces. A sense of detail and the human scale of the public open spaces create an inviting and involving sense of place. This, in turn, helps enrich the city experience for those who live and work in the surrounding neighborhood, as well as for citizens of the city of Oakland as a whole.

The need to create community also lies behind the 1987 design for the Graduate School of International Relations and Pacific Studies at the University of California, San Diego. Rather than a single large building, KMD created a multistructure campus. This facilitated the creation of humanly-scaled cloisters and plazas evocative of traditional academic settings. Similarly, the 1992 California Polytechnic University Business Administration and Education Building renovation and addition was based on the development of a medieval cloister, with the effect of promoting increased collegiality among students and faculty.

In KMD's commercial projects, the effort to revitalize the urban fabric and promote a sense of place and human scale has produced vital and unique solutions such as St. Francis Place in San Francisco and One Colorado Boulevard in Pasadena.

St. Francis Place is a high-rise housing project developed over a retail base. The housing itself is divided into buildings of differing scale so that the larger structures do not dominate. Towers are pulled back into the site so that the street image of the project is one of lower density retail and residential. Within the project, low-rise housing and townhouses balance off the larger apartment towers.

One Colorado Boulevard brings together retail, restaurant, office, and entertainment in a project that combines the renovation of historically significant buildings with the development of new structures. One Colorado is an example of how KMD brought its understanding of urban context and human scale to a renovation project. By transforming a little-used space into a lively, vital and commercially active core, KMD not only inspired intense use, but also furthered sensitive development in the area around the site.

KMD has long been noted not only as a firm that is able to create projects in tune with their context, but also as a firm able to "think like a developer." This unique synthesis is highlighted by projects that achieve maximum-per-square-foot profitability through the appropriate mix of spaces, uses, and environments. The bottom line is simply this: Spaces that people like to visit and that enhance the humanity of an area, are places people want to live, work, play, and shop.

The firm's success in creating workable and exciting mixed-use urban projects has been a catalyst for further commissions to design major urban centers both in the U.S. and elsewhere. Recently completed Nadya Park in Nagoya is an example of how a project can bring together a number of complementary commercial, office, and artistic uses in a large community project center. The heart of the project is a large public gathering space, part crossroads, part town square. At the same time, the project has served to promote Nagoya's rising status as a design and merchandising center.

NADYA PARK
NTERNATIONAL DESIGN CENTER

Similarly, the Kookmin Bank headquarters building in Seoul focuses much of its energy on the public plaza fronting the buildings, as well as on incorporating a number of public functions into the design of the building itself. The result is a design with highly visible, easily accessible public functions set in a dramatic, open environment, within a competition-winning high-rise tower. When completed, the Kookmin Bank will not only be among the tallest buildings in Asia, it will also provide one of the most accessible public spaces in South Korea.

KMD was also an early advocate of applying the principles of asset management to its urban projects. Because of its ability to balance development projects with institutional and corporate work, KMD can apply a developer's mentality to the analysis of its clients' real-estate investments.

Through this approach, the firm is helping clients find tremendous hidden value in large-scale planning projects. This insight is being applied to assisting California municipalities including Palo Alto, San Francisco, Oakland, and Pasadena with their own asset management strategies. This includes a review of the viability of reusing facilities, selling buildings, relocating certain uses, and in general developing a long-term plan for urban real-estate investments.

Designing places that exude vitality and a sense of well-being makes good sense from a business point of view and provides a basis for strong design. In short, spaces defined by sensitive design work well for users, passersby, and owners. As can be seen by the following designs, KMD has been able to take on a vast array of different kinds of urban and campus projects, often with difficult site and use constraints, and consistently create buildings that exemplify livability, human interaction, and a highly developed sense of community and place.

In the end, KMD interprets modern architecture as an art that brings people together, rather than further alienating them. It sees design as a way to promote a sense of community and human scale. And it recognizes that success is defined by an ability to reinforce the connection between buildings and people and by acting on the notion that successful, vital buildings and campuses enliven their context and celebrate the richness and complexity of modern life.

KOOKMIN BANK
HEADQUARTERS BUILDING

MORNING PARK CHIKARAMACHI RETIREMENT COMMUNITY

NAGOYA, JAPAN

Welcoming residents and visitors alike with a curving entrance that pays homage to Nagoya's whitewashed Tokugawa-era Samurai houses, Morning Park Chikaramachi Retirement Community is a 60,000-square-foot (5,400-square-meter) complex that seeks to redefine the notion of Japanese apartment design. Instead of the typical solution of a single mid-rise residential tower, the project is conceived as a welcoming campus with two five-story buildings built around a courtyard garden that serves as a central meeting place and recreational area for Morning Park residents.

Working with client and associate architect, Kajima Corporation, KMD began by researching the needs of Japanese seniors, convening neighborhood meetings to gauge the importance of elements like open space, privacy, and access. Local residents, a little startled at first to be polled on their needs and desires, responded warmly to the exercise. While much of this research was used to design Morning Park Chikaramachi, a number of unprecedented concepts were incorporated into the project as well.

1   AERIAL VIEW SHOWING VAULTED ROOFS AND TILE WALLS
    HARMONIZING WITH EXISTING NEIGHBORHOOD

2   IN THE INTERIOR COURTYARD A SIMPLE WATERFALL UNITES
    JAPANESE AND WESTERN GARDEN TRADITIONS WITH ITS
    RADIATING BANDS OF GRANITE.

2

3

3   THE ENTRYWAY FROM THE COURTYARD WITH ITS
    CURVED WALL, DRAWS PEOPLE IN AND PAYS HOMAGE
    TO NEIGHBORHOOD WHITE-WALLED HOUSES.

4   METAL GRILLWORK REFLECTS TRADITIONAL JAPANESE STYLE.

5   HOUSING UNITS AND PUBLIC SPACES TAKE ADVANTAGE OF
    LIGHT AND AIR PROVIDED BY THE OPEN COURTYARD.

4

5

6   LAYERS OF DETAILING CONTRIBUTE TO THE VISUAL INTEREST OF THE
     COURTYARD FACADE.

9   CARVED STONE BENCH IN COURTYARD

10   FINE-GRAINED LANDSCAPING DETAIL OUTSIDE LIBRARY

7   WATER FEATURE DETAIL OFF COURTYARD

8   AN OLD ROOF TILE USED AS ONE OF THE ARRANGED ELEMENTS IN
     THE STONE GARDEN INCORPORATES NEIGHBORHOOD TRADITION.

8

7

9

10

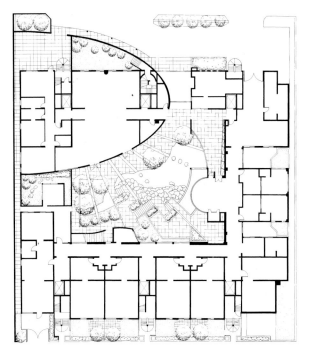

COURTYARD

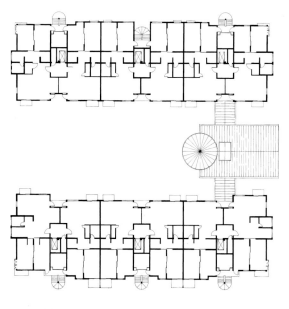

TYPICAL FLOOR

11

12

24

13

11 BRIDGE OVER ENTRANCE VESTIBULE AND LOUNGE AREA

12 DOUBLE-HEIGHT ENTRANCE VESTIBULE; GLASS WALLS, COOL MASONRY EXTERIOR, AND WARM CHERRY WOOD DOOR TRIM UNITE THE TRADITIONAL AND THE MODERN.

13 INTERIOR LIGHTING AND PAINTED CANVAS PROVIDE A WARM, INVITING GATHERING PLACE.

14 SHOJI SCREENS IN THE OAK-LINED MAIN DINING ROOM INTRODUCE A TRADITIONAL ELEMENT INTO A MOSTLY MODERN ENVIRONMENT.

14

15 ELIMINATING THE CORRIDOR ALLOWS LIVING SPACE TO
   FLOW THROUGH FROM STREET FRONT TO COURTYARD.

16 JUXTAPOSING RECTANGULAR BALCONIES AND CIRCULAR
   STAIRWAY ADD DETAIL TO THE SOUTH FACADE.

Where a typical Japanese apartment might have an entrance off a common corridor, the KMD design team chose to try an alternative approach to circulation by eliminating corridors on upper floors which all too often block views, waste space, and limit privacy. The solution was to place elevators in cores serving two apartments on each floor. Although at first it seemed that this approach would be more costly, conventional wisdom proved incorrect. By utilizing space typically devoted to corridors, an additional room was added to each apartment. Further, windows bring in natural light to each apartment from at least two sides. The scheme allows easy access to the common areas on the first two floors of the complex as well as to the highly prized courtyard space. Here, tea ceremonies and morning T'ai Chi Chuan help to create a sense of community for residents in a green space that is a welcome alternative to the streets and parking lots outside Morning Park Chikaramachi.

15

Looking southeast from the San Francisco/Oakland Bay Bridge, motorists are afforded a striking new vista focused on the twin towers of the 1.05-million-square-foot (90,000-square-meter) Oakland Federal Building. Occupying two square blocks and designed to accommodate four thousand employees, the twin eighteen-story Federal Building, completed in 1993, is a key element in the revitalization of Oakland's downtown and the largest Bay Area office building erected in a quarter century.

In an effort to create a powerful gateway to downtown Oakland, KMD designers discarded the concept of a dramatic single tower high-rise in favor of the more contextual twin-tower scheme. The axis of the towers, the public plaza and framed views create a strong entry to Oakland's revitalized civic center.

The towers' octagonal form was created to resolve certain contextual disparities of the street grid and surrounding neighborhood. The building's form accommodates both the traditional orthogonal geometry of Oakland and the clashing diagonal grid of the adjacent City Center complex. Similarly, the Federal Building's stone palette of beige and white was chosen to pick up both the golden hues of the old Oakland Tribune Tower and the creamy whiteness of the Oakland City Hall.

Five-story low-rise buildings cluster around the towers, housing Federal Courts and a conference center, and offer a sensitive stepping-down to the surrounding neighborhood. The plaza between the towers is split into two zones: a sunny piazza-style gathering space adjacent to the conference/auditorium wing and a more formal garden area that serves as the forecourt to the courthouse.

A potential controversy over an existing right-of-way along the 13th Street corridor, which runs through the middle of the Federal Building's central rotunda, was avoided by an innovative design compromise. Huge doors were crafted for the front and rear of the rotunda, which when opened provide a view corridor and pedestrian access through the center of the ornate metal clad and prismatic glass-enclosed five-story rotunda.

4

3

5

2 THE CENTRAL DOORWAY IN THE FEDERAL BUILDING ROTUNDA ACTS AS BOTH AN ENTRYWAY AND A THOROUGHFARE—A CREATIVE SOLUTION TO A RIGHT-OF-WAY CONUNDRUM.

3 WITH THE DOORS CLOSED, THE ROTUNDA STILL PROVIDES A LIGHT, OPEN VIEW BETWEEN THE TWIN TOWERS.

4 THE MASS OF THE TOWERS IS REDUCED BY CHAMFERING THE BUILDING'S SHAPE AT THE UPPER LEVELS.

5 LATTICE ROTUNDA ROOF

7

6   ROTUNDA WITH GATES OPEN;
    FACING WEST TOWARDS THE BAY

7,8   UPPER ROTUNDA CORRIDOR

9   ROTUNDA ROOF

9

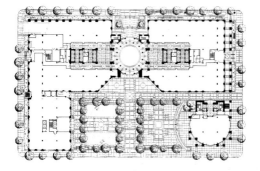

SITE

10 COURTROOM INTERIOR; MODERN YET DIGNIFIED

11 PUBLIC AUDITORIUM ON THE PLAZA LEVEL

12 EVENING VIEW OF OAKLAND'S NEW LANDMARK

10

11

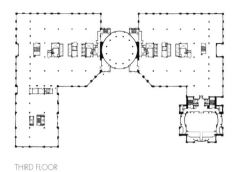

THIRD FLOOR

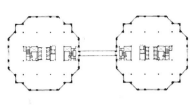

TYPICAL TOWER WITH BRIDGE

12

K.K. NAKAZATO CORPORATE HEADQUARTERS

TOKYO, JAPAN

In Tokyo's Shibaura District, along a waterfront that once bustled with the arrival and departure of sailing ships, the glass and aluminum K.K. Nakazato Corporate Headquarters pierces the sky with the imagery of a billowing mainsail. Nakazato's strikingly original design derives from KMD's charge, in collaboration with associate architect, Toda Corporation, to bring American insight to the design representing this traditional Japanese company. The structure's maritime theme symbolizes local history and creates an appropriate image for Japan's foremost importer of glassware, dinnerware, linen, and cutlery.

The three-sided 35,000-square-foot (3,150-square-meter) landmark, completed in 1992, houses corporate offices, a circular second-floor showroom and cafeteria, and a top-floor executive office with balcony and panoramic views of the harbor. By designing a void in the curtain wall to allow for a seventh-floor balcony, KMD architects took advantage of Tokyo's more liberal height allowance for signage. Without this break in the facade, the extended glass membrane would have been considered part of the structure and surpassed the city's strict building height requirements. As it is, the additional height adds to the building's nautical fluidity.

1 SIGN AS DESIGN; BY CREATING A VOID IN
THE CURTAIN WALL TO ALLOW FOR THE
SEVENTH-FLOOR BALCONY, THE DESIGN
TAKES ADVANTAGE OF TOKYO'S MORE
LIBERAL HEIGHT ALLOWANCE FOR SIGNAGE.

2 STREET SIDE, INTERSECTING CURVED FORMS

3 NAKAZATO BY NIGHT

THIRD FLOOR

SECOND FLOOR

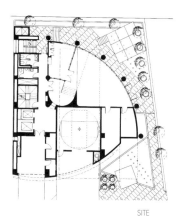

SITE

The allusion to unfurled sails is accomplished by a curving glass facade, mast-like columns, and a sloping roof line. The lyrical curve of the building's glass curtain wall also represents the results of design and materials analysis to determine which materials would be most resistant to the wind and salt of this waterfront environment. To further enhance maritime imagery, the staircase leading from the street to the second floor is designed as a ship's gangway. Details reinforce the imagery: the staircase crosses over a garden moat, its handrails mimic a ship's railings, and rope-patterned steel cables suspend the staircase from the building.

The poetic seafaring imagery also carries over to the building's structural system. Columns forming the periphery of the grid are emphasized by vertical red-painted trusses to enhance the overall impression of lightness and strength.

Nakazato Corporation is one of a number of progressive companies to move into Tokyo's intimate, canal-patterned waterfront area, a development created in conjunction with the city's plan to improve public access to this historic district.

4 NAUTICAL DETAILS INCLUDE STAIRCASE AS
   GANGPLANK; HANDRAILS AS SHIP'S RAILING,
   SUSPENDED BY ROPE-LIKE CABLE.

5 WARM WOOD AND MODERN STEEL;
   INTERIOR DETAIL

6 INTERIOR DETAILS AT NIGHT

7 SHOWROOM

5

6

7

9

8   VIEW FROM BALCONY ACROSS THE CANAL

9   SKYWARD, NAUTICAL IMAGERY AND SHAPES ABOUND

10 RED-PAINTED TRUSSES ENHANCE THE OVERALL IMPRESSION
    OF LIGHTNESS AND STRENGTH

10

SCHOOL OF INTERNATIONAL RELATIONS AND PACIFIC STUDIES

Creating a sense of community was the primary mandate for the 1987 commission to build a new home for the Graduate School of International Relations and Pacific Studies. Located on a bluff overlooking the Pacific Ocean on the western edge of campus the IRPS site was distinctive and apt for a school charged with the study of issues relating to nations located along the Pacific Rim. Working with the firm of Clark Beck & Associates as architect of record, KMD developed a unique community building solution to the design of IRPS.

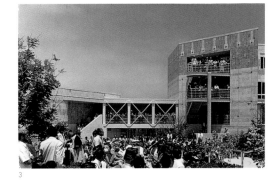

3

2

4

1   ENTRANCE TO CAMPUS VIA PEDESTRIAN WALKWAY
     LEADING TO CENTRAL PLAZA

2   CEREMONIAL STAIRCASE PROVIDES AN INFORMAL
     MEETING PLACE WITH A VIEW OF THE PACIFIC.

3   CENTRAL PLAZA AT GRADUATION; ILLUSTRATES THE
     CREATION OF SPACE THAT PEOPLE WILL USE FOR
     IMPORTANT CELEBRATIONS

4   BUILDING FORMS AND STAIRWAYS HELP DEFINE
     THE IRPS CAMPUS.

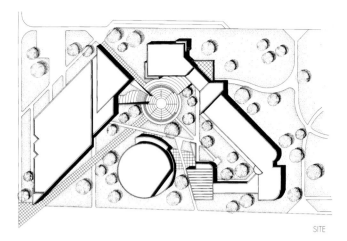

SITE

5   IRPS AT NIGHT; A PLACE RATHER THAN A BUILDING

6   THE AUDITORIUM IS A BACK DROP FOR THE DRAMA OF
       A NEW COMMUNITY AND A CELEBRATORY GATHERING
       SPACE ON CAMPUS.

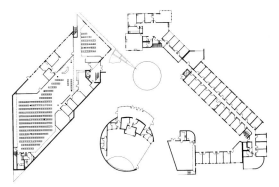

FIRST FLOOR

6

5

Rejecting the notion of a single structure to house the school, KMD designers conceived a 66,000-square-foot (5,940-square-meter), three-building campus-within-a-campus. The argument was compelling: A multibuilding site would give IRPS an enhanced sense of physical place as well as allow the shaping of humanly-scaled exterior cloisters and plazas evocative of traditional academic settings. KMD studies also illustrated that such usable exterior spaces are sorely lacking on most college campuses.

The three IRPS buildings, containing classrooms, research space, faculty offices, a library, computer lab and auditorium, were shaped around a series of courtyards, cloisters, and an amphitheater. The effect was to create a spatial focus and a setting that invited students and faculty to meet and interact as a community.

Highly pleasing to administrators were the construction economies that came from placing like functions together, in specifically designed structures. By separating, for example, auditorium from office space, the more stringent fire code requirements for assembly spaces were confined to fewer buildings.

The reduction in per square foot cost this strategy created allowed the inclusion of amenities that might not have been affordable if IRPS had been confined to a single building. Among the most pleasing of these is a facade of Jerusalem stone, the first used in America, giving the campus its distinct Mediterranean reflectivity.

7

SCHOOL OF INTERNATIONAL RELATIONS AND PACIFIC STUDIES, UCSD

8

9

10

11

7   IRPS AS SEEN FROM A MAJOR CAMPUS THOROUGHFARE OVERLOOKING
     THE PACIFIC OCEAN

8   A VARIETY OF FACADE ELEMENTS AND BUILDING FORMS CREATE THE
     FEELING OF A CAMPUS VILLAGE UNIFIED BY RICH MATERIALS AND DETAILS.

9,10 DETAIL OF ACADEMIC WING; DRAMATIC PACIFIC COAST LIGHTING
     CAPTURED BY JERUSALEM STONE AND PORTUGUESE MARBLE

11   ARCHITECTURAL FORMS PRESENT VARYING FACADES; BREAKS DOWN
     MASS OF BUILDING.

BUSINESS ADMINISTRATION AND EDUCATION BUILDING,

CALIFORNIA POLYTECHNIC UNIVERSITY, SAN LUIS OBISPO

The 1992 renovation and addition to the Business Administration and Education Building began with the notion that modern American academic architecture often resembles what KMD design principal Herb McLaughlin has called "concrete spaceships that landed on earth without scorching the grass"— buildings with no relationship to other campus buildings or their larger context. Countering that tendency, the 115,000-square-foot (10,350-square-meter) Cal Poly project successfully honors the existing Spanish Mission-style campus architecture while defining an enlivened twentieth-century adaptation of a medieval cloister. The effect has been to promote academic and social interaction among students and faculty.

The design extends and celebrates one of the most important campus pathways by allowing circulation to continue unimpeded through a new glass-enclosed lobby, out through a covered walkway, and past the entrance of a new three-hundred seat lecture hall. By continuing the passageway to a newly designed portico, KMD gave the buildings a new and striking campus portal.

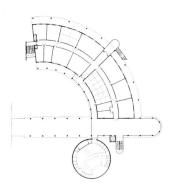

FIRST FLOOR

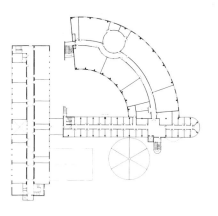

SECOND FLOOR

1   THE ADDITION AND RENOVATION CELEBRATE THE
    CAMPUS CONTEXT, WHILE CREATING AND HELPING
    TO DEFINE A CAMPUS EDGE.

2   CREATING IMPORTANT, USABLE EXTERIOR SPACE,
    INCLUDING A CLASSIC CLOISTER

3   COURTYARD AT SUNSET

By fashioning the addition's faculty and administrative offices, classrooms, and computer facilities along a curving axis, the building encloses a naturally sloping quadrangle, thus creating a new and highly focused commons space. With pillared galleries, palm trees, grassy slopes, and benches, this new, intimate, protected open space has taken on the manner of a traditional English academic cloister reinterpreted for a California campus in traditional California Mission style.

A KMD study of open space on college campuses illustrated that most campuses lacked well-defined, comfortable gathering places. This building responds to that need, serving as a campus meeting place of choice.

6

4

5

7

International Market Square gift and conference center was created through the rebuilding of an abandoned Munsingwear clothing factory, where the factory's four brick buildings were built between 1891 and 1912. The renovation, done in association with Winsor/Faricy Architects, one of the largest such projects in the United States, introduced the concept of urban "celebratory space" to Minneapolis. A bleak, industrial courtyard, used for loading railroad cars, was transformed into an atrium, where extraordinary popularity has transformed it into one of Minneapolis' most popular special events and banquet spaces.

The multifunctional atrium's three stages offer ample space for shows and entertainment. The detailing, featuring ironwork balconies and terraces, creates the illusion of a fanciful outdoor courtyard. A glass-encased elevator provides access to each level. The 685,000 square feet (61,650 sqaure meters) of space in the factory buildings was converted into more than two hundred showrooms.

1   CELEBRATORY "FOUND" SPACE, A PRIME PLACE TO PARTY IN MINNEAPOLIS

2   INDUSTRIAL COURTYARD PRIOR TO RENOVATION

3   THE PROCESS OF TRANSFORMING NEGLECTED SPACE INTO CELEBRATORY PLACE

4   AN ASPIRING TOWER IN THE MIDST OF HORIZONTALITY

2

3

4

5

6

SECTION

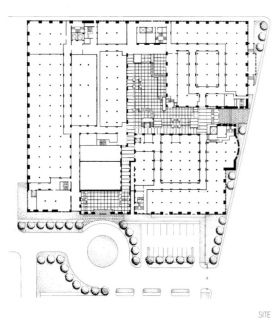

SITE

7

8

5   COMPLEX PRIOR TO RENOVATION

6   THE OLD LOADING DOCK IS NOW A UNIFYING PUBLIC SPACE
AND DRAMATIC LOBBY.

7   A "FOUND" SPACE BECOMES "THE" PLACE, AND GENERATES
UNEXPECTED INCOME IN THE PROCESS.

8   ARCHED FORMS GREET VISITORS AT FRONT RECEPTION LOBBY.

9   A WEALTH OF SPACES AND VIEWS CAN LEAD TO A MULTITUDE
OF SINGULAR EXPERIENCES.

9

Echoing the residential skyscrapers of New York City's Central Park, the twenty-seven-story, ninety-seven-unit Wilshire luxury residential tower has a deeply pitched copper roof, numerous balconies, and a facade both rich and varied. These are just a few of the interior and exterior details that made this the most successful—and highest earning—new building to come on the market in its era. Completed in 1990, with Richard Magee Associates as architect of record, the Wilshire incorporates a number of residential high-rise innovations, including individual elevator lobbies for all units and floor plans in which unit sizes vary at different levels of the building. These features, along with a private club and wine cellar, contribute to a 97 percent net-to-gross efficiency, lower construction costs, and faster sales.

Designed for a highly visible site on Wilshire Boulevard, the building makes extensive use of balconies and glass-enclosed conservatories on the lower levels to admit natural light and to take advantage of panoramic views stretching from Century City to Beverly Hills and Westwood.

Inside the Wilshire's entry gate is a formally landscaped, French-cobblestone-paved court which leads to a two-story lobby finished in marble and polished granite with mahogany paneling. The lobby floor is honed, pale cream limestone surrounding an elaborately inlaid rosette of pink and gold marble. Valet parking is available in a three-level, below-grade garage. The lower two floors include two-story town houses with large private gardens. A health club shares the first level and features a swimming pool, exercise facilities, weight room, party room, and an outdoor garden. Upper level units offer double-height living rooms with fireplaces in both the living room and master bedrooms. Two-story penthouses with large terraces occupy the Wilshire's top floors.

By dispersing elevators through the building, lengthy corridors leading from a central bank of elevators to the apartments were eliminated, replaced with a sense of privacy, privilege, and exclusivity.

3

2

1   FRONT ELEVATION FROM ENTRANCE COURT

2   FRENCH COBBLESTONES LEAD TO A TWO-STORY LOBBY.

3   THE VARIETY OF UNIT SIZES WAS POPULAR WITH BUYERS.

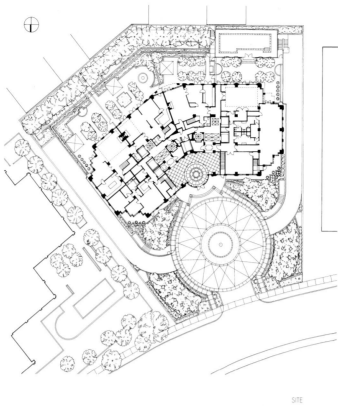

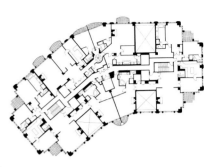

LOWER TIER

SITE

4   THE WILSHIRE, ONE OF LOS ANGELES'S
    LUXURY ADDRESSES

5   DUPLEX PENTHOUSE WITH A DOUBLE HEIGHT
    BALCONY CROWNS THE WILSHIRE.

6   A CENTRAL PARK–LIKE VIEW OF LOS ANGELES

4

5

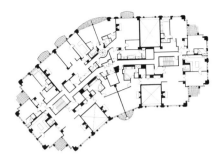

MIDDLE TIER

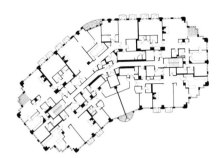

UPPER TIER

6

ROYAL WASHINGTON HOTEL

HIROSHIMA, JAPAN

1 THE ROYAL WASHINGTON'S DRAMATIC SPIRES PAY
HOMAGE TO THE KABUTO, A TRADITIONAL HELMET
WORN BY SAMURAI WARLORDS, SYMBOLIZING
LEADERSHIP, INDIVIDUALITY, AND PROSPERITY.

2 A LANDMARK TOWER ON THE HIROSHIMA
NIGHTTIME SKYLINE

3 NIGHTTIME; DRAMATIC JAPANESE SPIRES RISING
OUT OF A TRADITIONAL FRENCH MANSARD ROOF

Rising 23 stories above Hiroshima's Heiwa Odori, or Peace Boulevard, the KMD-designed Royal Washington Hotel represents the city's first major building by an American architectural firm. The classic tripartite structure features a highly articulated base, shaft, and mansard-roofed top. Completed with Tokyo-based ICW as associate architect, the Royal Washington is Japan's largest business hotel, containing 270 guest rooms, restaurants, ballrooms, a Shinto-style wedding chapel, and a "festival garden" featuring a multilevel cascading water sculpture.

Completed in 1992, the Royal Washington Hotel stands out with its roof line punctuated with dramatic spires that pay homage to the Japanese *kabuto*, a traditional helmet worn by Samurai warlords, symbolizing leadership, individuality, and prosperity. The design fully balances elements of ancient Japanese tradition with Western building articulation.

The design offers a fresh cultural perspective on design issues, particularly in regard to the Japanese tradition of keeping public and private space separate. Prior to the Royal Washington, mandated public spaces were often designed as plazas. Typically these faced heavily trafficked streets and discouraged potential users with sterile, cold, and often windblown conditions, given the relatively harsh climate of the region. At the Royal Washington the public and private spaces mesh through the design of "Grace Court."

4

5

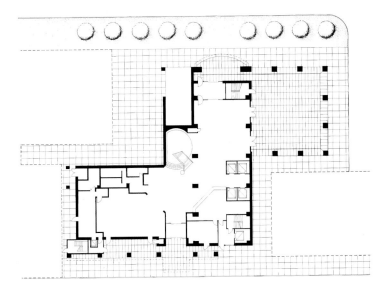

GROUND FLOOR

TYPICAL FLOOR

6

Using information from its Urban Agora study, KMD persuaded local planning authorities that a public space would be far more useful if it worked more like an outdoor room. The interior public space fronting the garden features a four-story waterfall, designed to compliment and balance the exterior water sculpture.

The Royal Washington's new-style plaza not only accommodates wedding receptions and special events, but also acts as an informal, and increasingly popular, public thoroughfare between Heiwa Odori and the adjacent entertainment district. The Royal Washington's urban celebratory gathering space was a first for Hiroshima and an innovation that successfully transcends traditional, and often constraining, local design standards.

7

1

The competition-winning design for the Kookmin Bank Headquarters, through its dramatic size (it will be the tallest building between the Han River and the North Pole), its gracious public plaza and thirteen-story atrium, reaffirms the prominence of the district of Seoul north of the Han River. Bisecting the Korean peninsula, the Han River has historically represented the division between new and old Seoul. North Seoul, home to Korea's established business headquarters and governmental institutions, in recent years has been eclipsed by newer corporate headquarters, rapid development, and several substantial office towers south of the river.

When completed in the year 2000, not only will the Kookmin Bank help reestablish the balance between north and south Seoul, but its state-of-the-art intelligent building systems, advanced design and materials, and interactive information systems will revolutionize the retail and customer service functions of Korea's largest national bank.

Function is key to the form of this 1.6-million-square-foot (488,700-square-meter) facility, designed in collaboration with Hee-Rim A/E Seoul. The forty-story tower holds the bank's high-security operations and administration areas, while the retail functions and public access uses are accommodated in the large floor plates of a horizontal podium. Eight floors of public access functions serve as a podium and are interconnected by a grand atrium and a series of escalators and elevators. Creative planning solutions led to a low coverage/high plaza ratio increasing the setback angle from 1:1.6 to 1:1.75, thus allowing three more floors to be added to the tower.

The civic importance of the project is celebrated through the expansive public plaza backed by a clear-glass, 120-foot (36-meter) curtain wall that creates a lively dialogue between public banking and outside urban activities. Auditorium and meeting rooms, which will serve both public and banking functions, are clearly articulated as they penetrate the publicly accessed podium and provide a counterbalance to the private tower. The gentle curve and scale of the podium wall integrate the urban fabric of this dense district of Seoul. Reflecting their critical role as the banking system's nerve center, masonry-clad computer floors link the podium (public) and tower (private) and clear span the auditorium below.

Extending beyond a literal interpretation of the functional massing, design details take this bank beyond the staid appearance of its peers. The different areas of the tower are sandwiched with subtly varied transparencies of glazing and are articulated by the clean lines of stainless steel sunscreens. The atrium curtain wall and the multistory office reception area are built with structural steel. The cable railings and metal panels, coupled with interactive multimedia building control and information systems, further illustrate Kookmin Bank's confidence in the future.

2

1 AERIAL RENDERING OF SOUTH ELEVATION

   HIGHLIGHTING THE HIGH-SECURITY BANKING TOWER,

   PUBLIC ACCESS RETAIL BANKING CENTER,

   THE AUDITORIUM, AND THE GRAND PLAZA

2 VIEW OF THE RETAIL BANKING CENTER ATRIUM

3   THE SITING OF KOOKMIN BANK NORTH OF
    THE HAN RIVER

4   THE GENTLE CURVE OF THE PODIUM WALL
    SOFTENS THE EDGE OF THE STREET CORNER.

5   VIEW FROM A TYPICAL DEPARTMENT
    LOUNGE/RECEPTION AREA LOOKING WEST
    TOWARD PAGODA PARK AND CHANG
    KYUNG-PALACE SHRINE

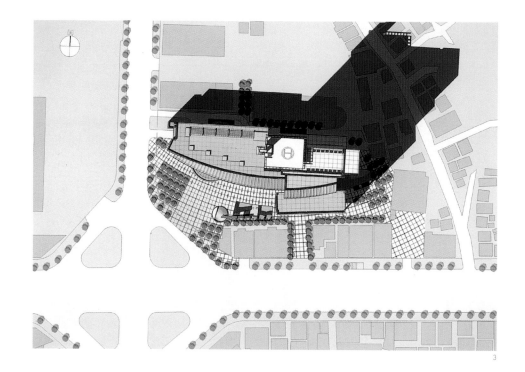

3

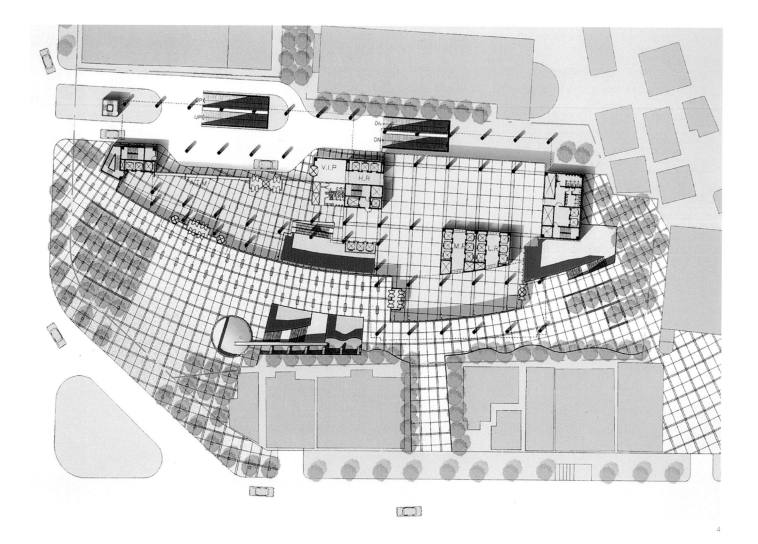

4

WASHINGTON/MONTGOMERY TOWER

SAN FRANCISCO, CALIFORNIA

1   GRANITE FINS ADD A HUMAN-SCALED ELEMENT TO THE
    LOWER LEVELS WHERE THE BUILDING MEETS THE STREET.

2   PROTECTED ENTRIES AND ARCHITECTURAL DETAILS ADD BOTH
    RICHNESS AND SCALE TO THE LARGE STRUCTURE.

3   AT STREET LEVEL, THE BUILDING CUTS BACK TO PROVIDE A
    PROTECTED ENTRY AND FOYER FOR THE RETAIL ACTIVITIES ON
    THE GROUND FLOOR.

4   ONE OF THE FIRST SINGLE BUILDING, MIXED-USE PROJECTS
    IN SAN FRANCISCO, THE WASHINGTON/MONTGOMERY
    TOWER IS CUT AWAY AT THE DIAGONAL OF COLUMBUS
    AVENUE TO PRESERVE THE VIEW ALONG ONE OF THE CITY'S
    FAVORITE INTERSECTIONS.

The first of a generation of mixed-use downtown high-rises, the twenty-six-story, 320,000-square-foot (28,800-square-meter) Washington/Montgomery Tower was a successful response to a key, and difficult, site in downtown San Francisco, where the financial district gives way to the historic North Beach neighborhood famous for its restaurants and small shops. Completed in 1984, the Washington/Montgomery Tower sits at a downtown intersection, directly across the street from San Francisco's landmark Transamerica Building.

Responding to a difficult urban context, the base of the tower was designed as a carefully detailed arcade. Kiosks and a ground-floor restaurant add human scale and visual interest at the pedestrian level and act as a gateway between Montgomery Street's financial high-rises and North Beach's eccentric accumulation of low-rise homes, shops, and offices. The design for the travertine floor of the arcade was carefully researched to provide richness and texture, while the honey-colored natural stone fulfilled the San Francisco Planning Commission's preference for light-toned exteriors that enhanced the city's Mediterranean look.

The upper floors of the tower, dedicated to thirty-three luxury condominiums, were designed as a highly articulated tribute to San Francisco's craggy, stepped skyline. Rounded solariums soften the tower's silhouette and offer some of the most dramatic and unobstructed views of the San Francisco Bay Area.

Key to the tower's articulated design was an attempt to address the popular perception that San Francisco's skyline was cluttered with too many stark, post-modern, "glass box" high-rises. Similarly, the building is dramatically cut away at the diagonal of Columbus Avenue, thus reinforcing the existing line and preserving views along one of San Francisco's most famous intersections.

Smaller cut-outs in the building extend down the other three corners. These form a transition between the airy upper floors and the more substantial office floors. The cut-outs also have the effect of providing numerous private balconies for the tower's offices, as well as responding to the strict planning goals of the City of San Francisco.

1

2

3

TYPICAL CONDOMINIUM FLOOR

TYPICAL OFFICE FLOOR

FIRST FLOOR

SITE

5

6

7

8

5   RESIDENTIAL UNITS FEATURE SPECTACULAR VIEWS OF
    SAN FRANCISCO'S VARIED TERRAIN AND ARCHITECTURE.

6   A POOL WITH A VIEW; THE LAP POOL FOR RESIDENTS
    CAPTURES SUN AND VIEWS FROM ITS HIGH-RISE LOCATION.

7   RESIDENTIAL UNITS INCLUDE GREENHOUSES THAT PROVIDE
    UNUSUAL LIGHT, AIR, AND VIEWS FOR HIGH-RISE HOUSING.

8   THE RESIDENTIAL UNITS ENJOY A SPARE BUT ELEGANT
    ENTRANCE LOBBY.

9   THE DYNAMIC FACADE BREAKS UP THE BUILDING'S MASS WITH
    CHAMFERED CORNERS USING GLASS AND DIFFERENT
    CLADDING TO MAKE A LARGE BUILDING SEEM LIGHT AND AIRY.

CENTRAL PLAZA

SAN FRANCISCO, CALIFORNIA

This office building was designed to provide a different composition from neighboring high-rises along San Francisco's lower Market Street area. The texture, detail, and proportions were designed to be richer and more traditional than surrounding structures built mostly in an adapted International Style during the 1960s. In addition to the rich texture of the building's facade, the design provides an open space that is partially enclosed by a low-rise wing of the building. It is this wing that fronts Market Street, providing a sun-filled break to the more densely developed high-rises fronting this busy street.

A special design feature of Central Plaza was that the building occupies two distinct but adjoining sites, yet it was required to provide a unified appearance and operational efficiencies. It was necessary to design the overall complex so that the property could be divisible in the future. Therefore, the low-rise and high-rise plan each has its own elevator core and lobby, but are connected by a shared lobby, accessed along a trellised pedestrian arcade that runs perpendicular to the street. This humanly-scaled arcade draws people into the complex and borders the open plaza.

This project provided a change of pace for the type of development that had been the norm along Market Street. Its plan, facade treatment, and low-rise element create a distinct image for the building. The plaza provides a comfortable gathering space and helps give the building a strong sense of place. As a result of these planning and architectural distinctions, Central Plaza has been fully occupied since its construction.

1   THE RICHLY TEXTURED FACADE FORMS A COMPLIMENTARY BRIDGE BETWEEN SAN FRANCISCO'S OLDER BUILDINGS AND NEWER, LESS ARTICULATED TOWERS.

2   AN ENTRANCE PORTICO CONNECTS THE TWO BUILDING ELEMENTS AND FORMS A HUMANLY-SCALED EDGE.

3   THE BUILDING STEPS BACK AND COMBINES A MIX OF DETAILS THAT FORM A DISTINCTIVE FACADE.

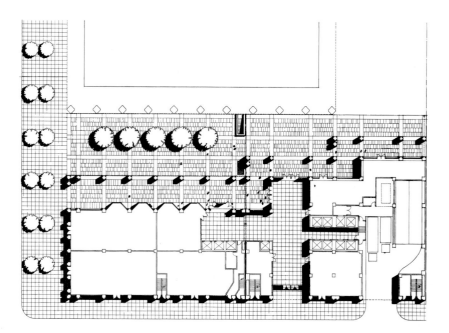

GROUND FLOOR

3—

Recalling the streamlined art deco high-rises of the Jazz Age, Sacramento's twenty-six-story Plaza Park Tower, completed in 1991, instantly became a downtown landmark in the California state capital. The 430,000-square-foot (38,700-square-meter) Plaza Park Tower was the crowning element of the development of an entire downtown Sacramento block; its design aimed at creating a building that would fit easily into its urban context.

The project's tripartite design allows the unification of several distinctive themes. Built adjacent to Sacramento's Carnegie Library, Plaza Park Tower's 60-foot (18-meter) base exactly matches the height of the historic building. At the same time, Plaza Park's soaring shaft and articulated top are set back to create the illusion of a building lighter and taller than it actually is. To emphasize the building's height, green-tinted windows are set vertically, while mullions run from the building's base to its top. At the top, the mullions terminate in fan-shaped forms recalling the peaks of Streamline Moderne high-rises. For added definition, these are lit at night with fiber-optic strips.

Clad in precast concrete, French limestone is used at both the top and bottom to give the building an added sense of lightness. To respond to the light terra-cotta and brick of adjacent buildings, KMD utilized a near pastel palette, except at the building's base, which is powerfully grounded by the use of Swedish Mahogany polished granite.

Plaza Park's soaring three-story lobby uses window walls along its full length to draw people inside, as well as to illuminate the artwork within. One interior wall features four allegorical murals painted by Richard Piccolo depicting important events in the history of the Sacramento Valley. The lobby's floor consists of geometrically patterned granite that reiterates both interior and exterior detailing. Two bronze cougars, designed by Gwynn Murrill, keep guard at the main entrance. Inside, restaurants and shops give the building's lobby a sense of destination and activity.

Plaza Park Tower's construction marked the first major high-rise created to respond to height limits and street setbacks defined by Sacramento's pioneering downtown planning guidelines, which KMD helped develop. These emerged in response to the City of Sacramento's concern for accommodating future growth while maintaining a respect for its older buildings.

As part of the Plaza Park development, KMD also created the design to renovate the nearby Carnegie Library, as well as existing parks in front of the buildings and across the street.

1   THE PLAZA PARK AT DUSK, FITTING INTO ITS
    URBAN CONTEXT

2   THE PLAZA PARK'S DETAILS HARK BACK TO
    THE AGE OF ART DECO.

2

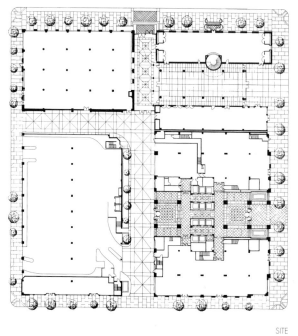

SITE

3   AN EXCITING VOLUME OF SPACE, THE BUILDING IS DETAILED IN
     POLISHED GRANITE.

4   THE ENTRANCE FEATURES A THREE-STORY ATRIUM WITH MURALS
     DEPICTING SACRAMENTO'S HISTORY.

4

SHANGHAI INTERNATIONAL BUSINESS CENTER

SHANGHAI, CHINA

Shanghai is on the verge of a new period of domestic and international prominence, and KMD believes the city's architecture should reflect the spirit of this new era. KMD recently won an international competition for the design of two large mixed-use projects in China: The Shanghai International Business Center and the New Shanghai International Plaza, both scheduled for completion in 1999. Although the projects are in separate neighborhoods, each creates a sense of place by accommodating many levels of activity and interest.

The Shanghai International Business Center consists of a 60-story landmark office building connected via an atrium to a 450-room, four-star hotel and an 850,000-square-foot (76,500-square-meter) retail center. Set on 10 acres (4 hectares) in the upscale Xi Hui district, the project also includes a 500,000-square-foot (45,000-square-meter) apartment/office complex and a 1,500-space parking facility. The central civic plaza anchors the buildings and provides a connection to a park on the north side of the complex. The project will be linked with Shanghai's many districts via a new subway system.

KMD's design intermingles references to Western culture, such as urban open space and modern architectural forms, with Chinese tradition expressed through the use of natural settings. This combination of elegant architecture and beautiful landscaping provides a visual balance for pedestrians, who can stroll through indoor/outdoor summer and winter gardens, across a quaint footbridge linked to the park, or up and down terraced garden steps.

1 SHANGHAI INTERNATIONAL BUSINESS
CENTER CONCEIVED FROM THE BUND

2 A MASSING STUDY OF THE CENTER'S
NEIGHBORHOOD

3 PEDESTRIAN TRAFFIC FLOWS BETWEEN THE
CENTER AND THE PARK ACROSS THE STREET.

4

SHANGHAI INTERNATIONAL PLAZA

SHANGHAI, CHINA

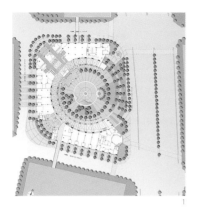

1　A CURVILINEAR BROW COMPLEMENTS THE PATH OF THE HUANG PU RIVER.

2　LANDMARK TOWER PAYS TRIBUTE TO SHANGHAI'S DIVERSITY.

3　WITHIN THE PLAZA, THE TOWER FACES THE HEART OF SHANGHAI.

4　RETAIL AND ENTERTAINMENT SPACES ARE ARRANGED IN A LAYERED, CIRCULAR PATTERN AROUND THE PLAZA.

Across town, in a Shanghai historic district known as "the Bund," the 1.5-million-square-foot (135,000-square-meter) New Shanghai International Plaza rises from the landscape. KMD drew inspiration for the facility's design from "Majestic Peaks," a 1706 Shaitao Ji poem that pays homage to the thousand peaks of green and azure of China's Yellow Mountains. The distribution of mass and the vertical articulation of the towers offers a dignified interpretation of this eternal landscape.

Also organized around an urban plaza, this project features a landmark office tower at its northwest axis, with corporate banks as its anchor tenants. Retail and entertainment spaces arranged in a layered, circular pattern around the plaza. The outer ring includes a concentric pedestrian walkway, complete with shaded arcades for merchant displays. It also is an ideal setting for street fairs and open produce markets. The middle layer consists of a galleria and specialty retail shopping atrium. The central plaza blends an amphitheater and festival stage with private seating.

KMD's arrangement of the International Plaza's buildings is a tribute to the diverse elements of Shanghai, with the landmark tower, which faces the heart of the city, its visual highlight. The facade of another tower rising from the community plaza salutes the new Nan Pu Bridge, a symbol of modern strength and technology. The project's curvilinear brow stresses the view of the Bund and development of Pudong, while complementing the path of the Huang Pu River.

Both the New Shanghai International Plaza and the Shanghai International Business Center were financed by Shanghai International Trust and Investment Corporation.

2

3

4

PURI JAYA
CENTRAL BUSINESS DISTRICT
MASTER PLAN

TANGERANG, INDONESIA

The Jayaland Master Plans were a 1994 competition winner for the design of the central business district for two new Indonesian cities. KMD architects began by establishing a set of principles that simultaneously form a strong underpinning for the design process and provide a necessary flexibility utilizing existing site characteristics to develop integrated, indigenous, and sustainable living/working environments.

Set within an overall village/residential master plan conceived by Calthorpe/Solomon, Associated Architects and Planners, the KMD plan for the central business districts weaves together a core office/retail business district and perimeter retail/housing with shaded pathways and arcades. The plan's attempt was to ease vehicle traffic and encourage pedestrian and bicycle uses by providing ready alternatives motor vehicles.

One of the two proposed Jayaland sites, Puri Jaya, is planned as a city of 300,000 in Tangerang, an area of Java, an island lying west of Jakarta. Initial plans for a more formalized configuration for the 300-acre (120-hectare) downtown were refined early in the process in response to an awkwardly converging road net, a ring of villages and a canal cutting through the site, which made appropriate traffic and pedestrian circulation a challenge.

Although the developer initially expressed a preference for a town built on a straight-line axis, the KMD design team recognized that the existing roads, which entered the site at irregular angles, made this strict alignment impractical.

The KMD team decided on a circular pattern of residential development built around a central commercial zone. Although an existing canal precluded a completely circular design, a decision was made to develop a semicircular form south of the waterway that would maintain effective site circulation, organize land uses, and allow for the creation of landmark boulevards. The plan also introduced the notion of a "couplet system" of divided roadways. The separated roadways enhance the impression of grand arrival boulevards and allow traffic on the town's major roads to flow freely. This concept is a novel one in auto-choked Indonesian cities that have, for the most part, replicated the model of Jakarta with its main, unseparated streets creating unruly congestion.

Taking the separated roadways as primary spokes, the team then designed streets as concentric circles to create districts radiating out from the city's central open space. These ring roads act as delineators for differing uses, with a high-rise district in the inner core and mid-rise housing on the outermost ring acting as a buffer between downtown and the outlying villages. Shaded pedestrian walkways and arcades connect with corridors of retail throughout the Puri Jaya plan and act as the glue holding the business/retail/residential fabric of the plan together.

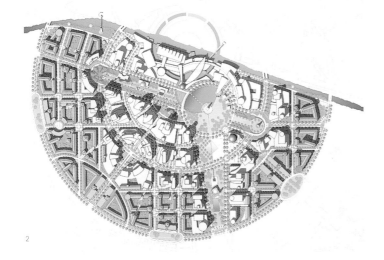

1 OVERALL SITE WITH CENTRAL BUSINESS DISTRICT

2 CONCENTRIC CIRCLES RADIATING WITHIN THE CENTRAL BUSINESS DISTRICT CREATE LANDMARK BOULEVARDS AND SIGNIFICANT BUSINESS ADDRESSES.

3 VIEW ACROSS THE CENTRAL BUSINESS DISTRICT

2

3

BUMI JAYA CENTRAL BUSINESS DISTRICT MASTER PLAN

SIDOARJO, INDONESIA

The second part of the Jayaland development, Bumi Jaya, is a 4,250-acre (1,700-hectare) development planned for the heart of Sidoarjo, Indonesia, a town located outside the city of Surabaya. Plans for the Bumi Jaya Central Business District embody the KMD-inspired notion of incorporating living and work spaces while striving to promote pedestrian travel and reduce street traffic.

Bumi Jaya's central business district is a complex, sensitively interwoven mix of commercial and retail space, with park-like, green, open-space networks and mid-rise residential structures at the perimeter acting as buffers for the surrounding residential fabric. The location of the office towers along opulent boulevards and tree-lined streets offers a prestigious location for business development.

KMD was chosen to design the Central Business Districts of the Jayaland projects largely because of the firm's solid reputation for creating innovative, multi-use urban spaces. The challenge of Bumi Jaya was to create user-friendly, living/working environments while seamlessly combining new development within an existing fabric of housing and light industry.

1

2

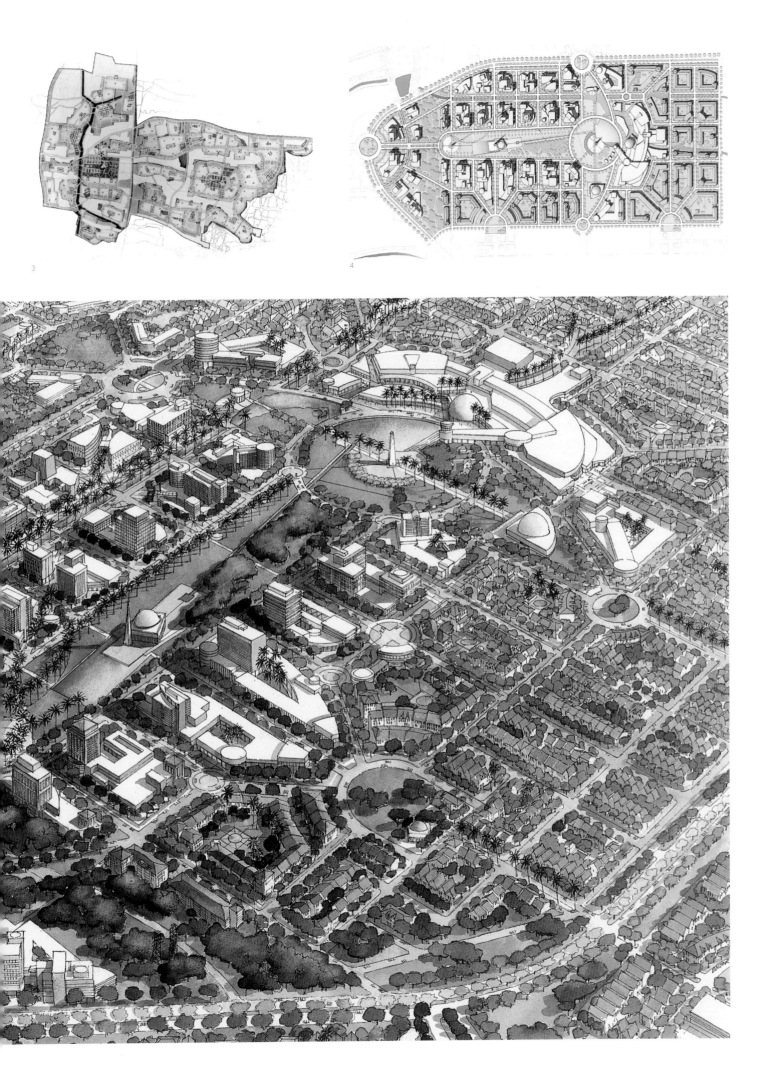

3

4

PERDANA RAIL CITY

KUALA LUMPUR, MALAYSIA

In the design of Perdana Rail City in Kuala Lumpur, KMD was faced with the challenge of creating an integrated mixed-use urban district built on a platform over existing railroad tracks. The design process became a critical exercise in urban vision; organizing a project with severe technical constraints, while at the same time creating a vital urban center. Planned for 180 acres (72 hectares) of what was formerly a train switching yard, the 13-million-square-foot (1.2 million-square-meter) project is intended to extend Kuala Lumpur's famous "golden triangle" district.

The project centers around a terminal building thematically designed to serve as the city's "great hall." This modern center, loosely fashioned after the artful train stations of a century ago, is both a communal meeting space and a connecting point for light rail, inter-city trains, commuter trains, buses, auto, and an air-rail link to an international airport at Sepang.

The various modes of transit are separated on different levels with alternate access points. The train station complex acts as the hub around which project traffic moves.

The major pathway for pedestrian traffic links the combined hotel and residential district on the south side with office buildings and more than four million square feet of retail space on the north, with the station complex located strategically in between. An adjacent office tower, the tallest element of the project, serves as a campanile and welcomes visitors by acting as the reference point for Perdana Rail City. The tower's spiral roof form was inspired by the minaret at the Great Mosque of al-Mutawakkil at Samarra.

To promote pedestrian use throughout this large complex a system of shade and ventilation is provided as a response to Malaysia's equatorial climate. The design achieves a comfort level for pedestrians through the use of natural elements: water features, screened walls, and lush foliage. Cascading public gardens, fountains, plazas, and indoor public spaces encourage pedestrians to explore the complex, its rooftop gardens, and other outdoor areas.

1   THE RAIL STATION PLAZA INTEGRATES DIFFERENT TRANSPORTATION, CIRCULATION, AND CONCESSIONS ON DIFFERENT LEVELS.

2   THE GRACEFUL ROOF CANOPY OF THE RAIL STATION IS INSPIRED BY THE MINARET AT THE GREAT MOSQUE OF AL-MUTAWAKKIL AT SAMARRA.

3   A STAND-ALONE MIXED-USE DEVELOPMENT BUILT ON A PLATFORM OVER A FIVE-LINE RAIL RIGHT OF WAY

4   LEMONADE OUT OF LEMONS; SEVERE SITE PLAN CONSTRAINTS LEAD TO A MORE WORKABLE DESIGN.

4

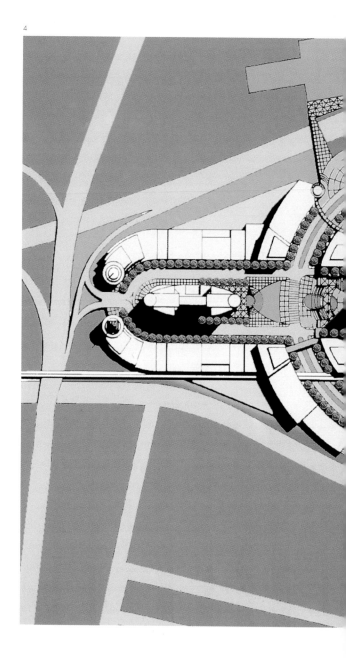

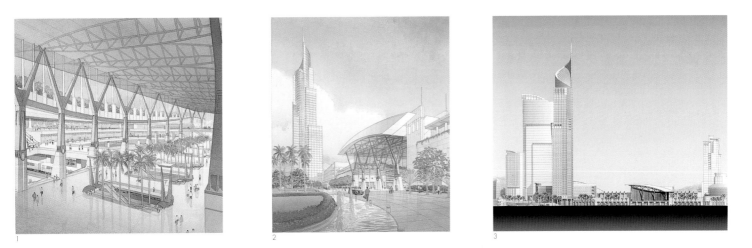

1

2

3

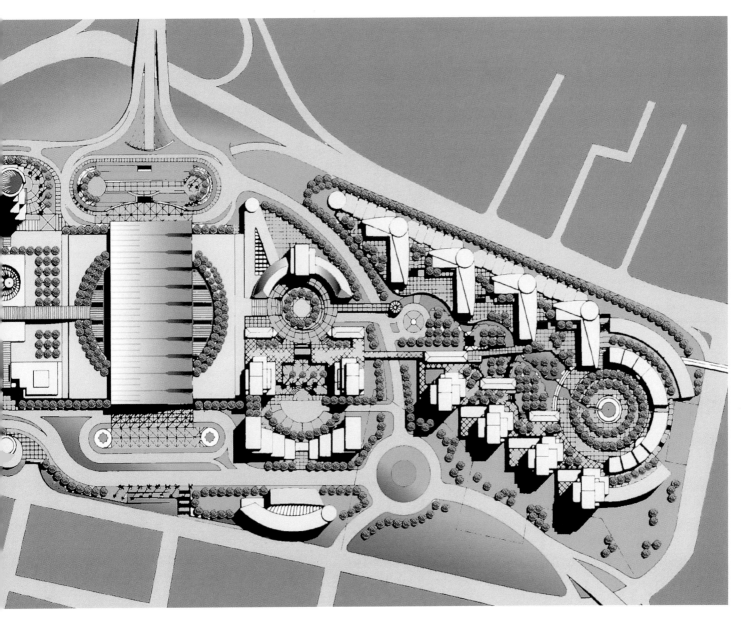

NADYA PARK
INTERNATIONAL DESIGN CENTER
NAGOYA, JAPAN

1   AERIAL VIEW WITHIN THE CONTEXT OF ITS NAGOYA
    NEIGHBORHOOD

2   NADYA PARK OFFERS A DRAMATIC NEW PRESENCE
    IN A WELCOME PUBLIC SPACE IN NAGOYA.

3   THE TOWERS OF NADYA PARK WOVEN INTO THE
    FABRIC OF JAPAN'S DESIGN CAPITAL

Playing an important role in the awakening Japanese cultural appetite for celebratory public spaces, the $350 million, 1-million-square-foot (90,000-square-meter) Nadya Park project in Nagoya is a retail, business, exhibition and multipurpose design and cultural center created to help re-enliven the heart of Japan's fourth largest city. Nadya Park is designed around two distinctive glass and polished aluminum-clad towers connected by a soaring atrium that now serves as one of the city's most important new public venues and as a backdrop for cultural life in a redeveloped site near the heart of historic Nagoya. Nadya Park integrates three distinct architectural elements to create both a dynamic interaction among retail and cultural elements. It is a bold announcement of Nagoya's emergence as Japan's design capital.

Completed in 1996 with Daiken Sekkai as collaborating architects, Nadya Park combines private and public use with its two towers. The 14-story public building contains a three-level design center with retail, display, and educational facilities, convention meeting rooms, a 700-seat theater, 300-seat multipurpose hall, and a youth center. The 23-story commercial tower houses specialty retail stores, showrooms, and restaurants on its bottom seven floors and offices above. The 7-story retail base of the larger tower is finely detailed and designed to reach out toward the street to excite and stimulate pedestrian access.

Designed to open southward towards Nagoya's adjacent Yaba Park, the Nadya Park project is also within close proximity to a major commercial boulevard to the east, an entertainment district stretching to the north, and a museum complex two blocks to the west. From its inception Nadya Park was envisioned as an important unifying feature for the city of Nagoya. With its international design and youth-oriented cultural centers, Nadya Park also serves as a catalyst for the rejuvenation of an important and central urban node.

4   THE MAIN ENTRANCE PROVIDES A LIGHT FILLED, ACTIVATED ENTRY, CLEAR ILLUSTRATION
     OF BUILDING USES, AND VIEWS OUT TO NAGOYA.

5   LIGHT FILLS THE ENTRY ATRIUM.

6   THE STRUCTURE, MECHANICS, AND A VARIETY OF USES ARE ALL EXPRESSED IN THE ATRIUM.

4

The two towers are connected by the 165-foot (50-meter) central atrium, the exposed frames, ducts, and structural details of which subtly repeat design elements from the two towers. Rather than columns, the atrium relies on spidery steel framing for structural support, giving it an airy, open feeling, the type of space well-suited for celebratory public gatherings.

Irregular balconies, open stairways, and a glass elevator provide the atrium with a number of different viewpoints, giving a sense of movement, detail, and human scale to such a large space. At distinct points along the connecting walls, the inner workings of the towers are exposed, giving passersby in the atrium glimpses of activities inside the buildings. This gives the atrium a sense of interactivity and the viewer an instinctive and informative understanding of the organization of the entire complex.

5

6

7 A WELCOMING ENTRY TO A LARGE, BOLD COMPLEX

8 ATRIUM SPACE EMPHASIZES OPENNESS, HIGH VISIBILITY AND EASE OF ACCESS.

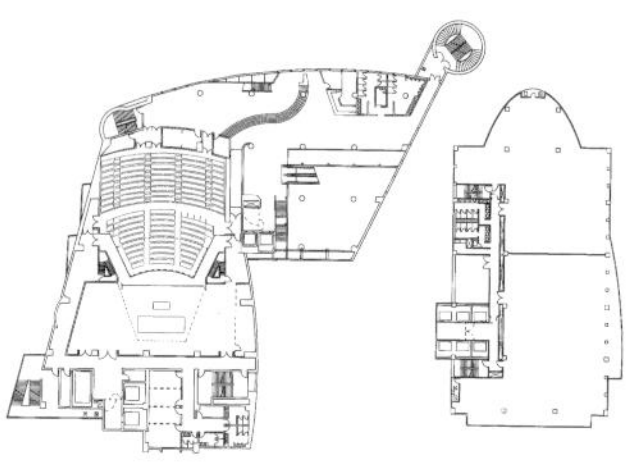

TENTH FLOOR

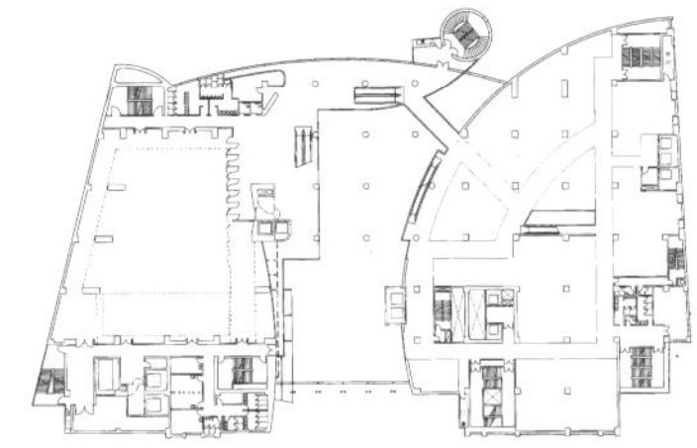

THIRD FLOOR

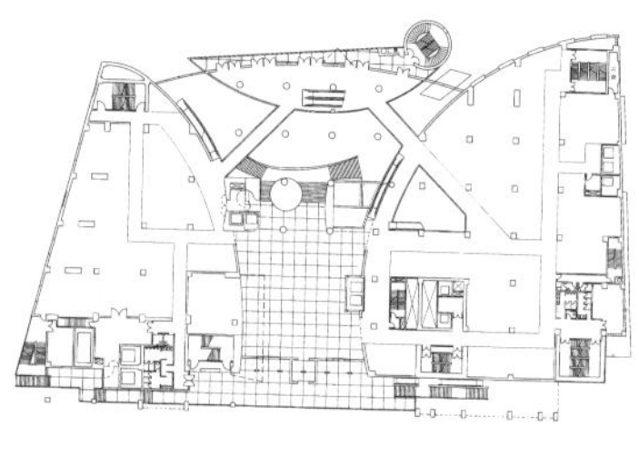

SECOND FLOOR

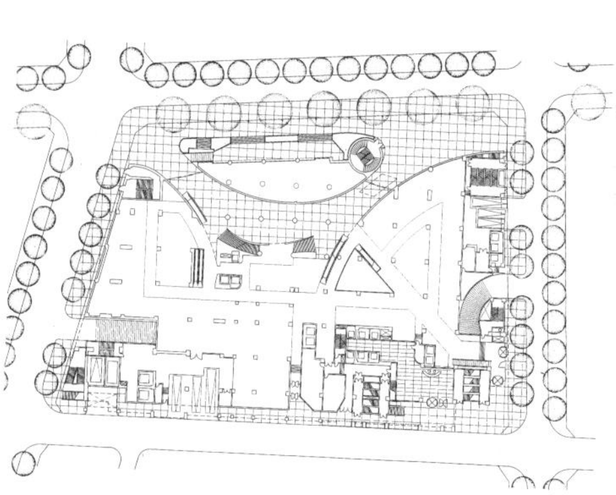

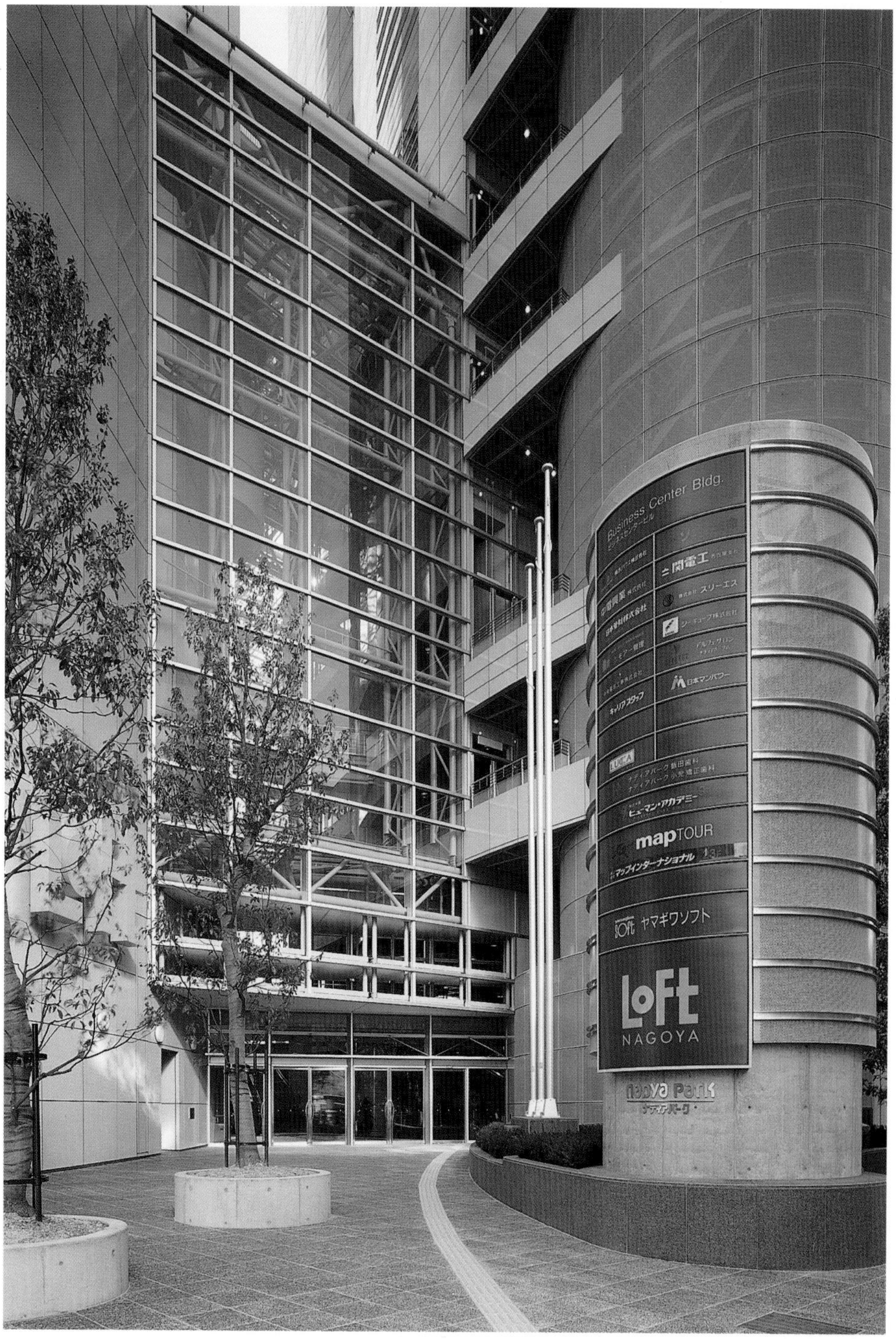

7

9

10   12

9   MEZZANINE LEVELS LINING THE CENTRAL ATRIUM CONNECT SHOPS
      AND PROVIDE AN EXCITING VANTAGE POINT AT EVERY TURN.

10   NATURAL LIGHT FILLS THE ENTIRE ATRIUM, HIGHLIGHTING DETAILS.

11   ELEVATOR LOBBY OFFERS SKY DECK VIEWS.

12   RETAIL SPACES DRAW PEOPLE IN FROM THE BUSY ATRIUM.

11

13 APPROACHING THE NADYA PARK SHOPS
    AND THEATER ENTRANCE FROM THE NORTH

14 A RICH PALETTE OF HIGH-TECH MATERIALS
    HIGHLIGHTS THE DESIGN ORIENTATION OF
    NADYA PARK.

15 SHADOW AND LIGHT PLAY ON THE DETAILS
    OF THE FACADE.

13

14

15

HEALTH CARE:
INQUIRY, INNOVATION, LEADERSHIP

Throughout much of this century, the traditional policies of medical care facilities frequently manifested themselves in massive buildings with a network of bleak, seemingly endless corridors. Intimidating and bewildering circulation routes weaving through noisy, high-pressure environments provide patients and staff with few opportunities for respite, contemplation, and reflection. With deeply set traditions of care delivery and a continuing focus on the remarkable advance of technology, the desire to reevaluate the patient's physical environment was overshadowed.

From its inception, KMD has sought to challenge the status quo of health-care design. The impetus for KMD's challenge, grounded in the firm's health-facility research in the mid-1960s. It is the firm's conviction that a positive relationship exists between the quality of the physical environment and the well-being of the confined patient, a major departure from the conventional model of "you stay in bed, the staff will make you well."

The revolutionary health-care design message that KMD began to spread is the fundamental relationship of the design to the healing processes, an architectural corollary to the maxim "patient, heal thyself." While it has been clear that design speaks to the hospital's image in the community, its public acceptance and financial competitiveness, it is the patient's immediate environment that remains critical to the healing process.

Architecturally, this meant the creation of hospital and health-care facilities where patients would be able to take responsibility for their own well-being in a place of warmth, calm and, whenever possible, with nature only a window or a courtyard away. Early KMD designs for health facilities featured open, airy nursing units with access to easily monitored, enclosed cloisters and gardens. There, supervised patients could expand their convalescent environment to the outdoors.

KMD was also an early innovator of the concept of the "medical village." Not only were separate buildings with specific uses more economical, but they were also places that modeled, in a controlled environment, a more normal living situation for patients. And by placing different functions in different buildings in a horizontal campus setting, later renovations could be accomplished in stages without shutting down large parts of the hospital.

Initial resistance to KMD's attempts to use the creation of place and celebratory space to promote "wellness" waned as the authoritarian medical model was challenged by patients, families, and doctors. A social sea change took place throughout the '70s and '80s as it became generally accepted that increased personal involvement could speed the healing process, which itself could be facilitated by a healthy place to heal. There was a broad level of success for this new healthcare paradigm. And with it came acceptance of innovations such as the "hospital street," wider, brighter corridors, lobbies and atriums that encouraged patients to be more active and engaged. These redesigns helped engender a feeling of greater well-being during the stressful intake process and through often painful medical procedures. And recognizing that different hospital activities induced different stress levels, among patients and family alike, KMD applied the concept of placemaking to the design of a hierarchy of lobbies, with differentiated designs, sizes, furnishings, and ambiance.

The successes were striking. At Brigham and Women's Hospital in Boston, for example, an unappealing pedestrian link mordantly referred to as "The Pike"(as in Massachusetts Turnpike) served as a necessary connection between buildings. KMD saw that this link could serve as a resource, a gathering space, and as a dramatic organizing feature. Redesigning the Pike produced an area so widely liked and heavily used that a national food and beverage chain offered the hospital significant rent-to-lease space in this new lobby area.

KMD also recognized that, while patients desire the security of a high-tech environment during treatment, they also crave the soothing settings of nature and home. This led to the concept of environmental "phasing" over the course of treatment; a neutral waiting area before a procedure, high-tech medical facilities during, and warm, homey recovery areas afterwards. KMD applied this concept of medical placemaking to one of the first "birthing centers" at Cottonwood Hospital Women's Center in Murray, Utah. Completed in 1984, this was one of the first facilities of its kind and a model for hundreds of subsequent birthing centers.

In a series of ongoing studies, KMD recognized that the needs of sick adolescents and children varied widely from those of adult populations. Firm designs for pediatric care facilities such as the Children's Health Center at Duke University and the Starbright Pavilion, planned for Los Angeles, were child-centric with scale, lighting, graphics, and amenities adapted to the sensibilities of younger patients.

Economic considerations also became an overriding concern for KMD's health-care projects. Recognizing that financial constraints would increasingly drive facilities design, the firm sought ways to streamline escalating operational and facility costs. These were the genesis of such KMD innovations as the triangular nursing unit, designed to allow two nursing stations to cover an entire floor, and "swing beds" located between units that could take up slack when one ward was busy while another was quiet. The triangular floor configuration won numerous awards for its economy of space and ability to accommodate many concepts for patient-focused care from team to primary nursing.

Facilities for the elderly and chronically ill present another great challenge. KMD's work at Hi-Desert Skilled Nursing Center in Joshua Tree, California, and planning studies for the replacement of the twelve-hundred-bed Laguna Honda Hospital in San Francisco resulted in design concepts both economical to build and operate and humanistic in terms of patient environment. In recent years, issues of operational efficiency and the return on investment in facilities and personnel have driven the firm toward new innovations often going beyond planning and design to address management and investment issues. An example of this included a KMD-generated redevelopment program for Grady Memorial Hospital in Atlanta to convert a massive 1954 building into an efficient, state-of-the-art hospital, pediatric pavilion, and ambulatory care center for half the cost of the replacement facility the hospital had considered. Nursing costs were significantly reduced by creating floors of contiguous inpatient care units of forty-one beds each in lieu of four inflexible, stand-alone units of twenty-four beds per floor.

As investment in facilities becomes more challenging to health-care providers, KMD's response has been to develop both asset management studies and new prototypes of health-care delivery. For their HMO client Kaiser Permanente, the firm planned and designed entire prototype campuses in Southern California that enable gradual growth though progressively larger additions. And for PruCare, Prudential's HMO, KMD developed a prototype for a primary care clinic based on a unique visits-per-year model.

In its search for better ways to involve users in the planning process, the firm has pioneered the use of the computer as an illustration and communication tool. KMD developed an interactive, computer drawing system for planning and design. Participants in planning sessions now have the capability to make planning suggestions that are immediately displayed on a large, high-definition screen. This use of technology allows on-site decision making to further streamline the design process. KMD also developed a unique computer application for quick graphic evaluation of the potential for conversion of existing facilities for use as primary care centers.

Future patterns of health care will vary from one place to another, just as they do today depending on location, culture, demographics, available resources, the priority given to health care, and the ability of a society to avail itself of global advances in medicine. KMD has already assisted clients in meeting these and other industry challenges through designs that have become prototypes for the future of ambulatory care, birthing centers, pediatric facilities, and highly portable, prefabricated health-care facilities.

KMD is at the vanguard of American firms designing health-care facilities overseas. The firm's research, analysis, and respect for cultures results in new facilities that borrow concepts of planning, operation, and technology from the United States.

The worldwide challenges faced in health-care planning and design in the next few years are manifold. There is the need for the most basic infrastructure in underdeveloped areas and for cost-efficient high-technology, high-touch facilities in the developed world. And as can be seen in the following projects, in these and other areas, KMD's tradition of placemaking, inquiry, innovation, and design excellence will help the firm continue as one of the leaders in health care architecture.

MARIN GENERAL HOSPITAL

GREENBRAE, CALIFORNIA

Inspired by Marin County's unique hill forms, color, and foliage, the prow-shaped, 1989 addition to the Marin General Hospital has been described as "a green ship on a course through green hills." Without a highly refined understanding of site context, professional requirements, and community dynamics, however, the course through the design and approvals process might have proven to be a project-sinking mine-field. Instead, the 100,000-square-foot (9,000-square-meter) addition that combines surgical, orthopedic, cardiac, intensive, and transitional care facilities with a new main entrance, lobby, food service, and elevator core, is a textbook collaboration between KMD and Marin General, one of its oldest clients. A staff- and patient-sensitive environment was realized and further enhanced using innovative construction methods of "green architecture."

1   NATURAL COLORS CORRESPOND TO HILLSIDES
    AND FOLIAGE.

2   DRAMATIC PROW-LIKE FORM OF THE TRIANGULAR
    NURSING UNITS

3   VIEW FROM THE OLD MAIN ENTRANCE; THE
    SETBACKS, TRELLISES, AND GLASS CORNERS
    MINIMIZE BUILDING'S OVERALL MASS.

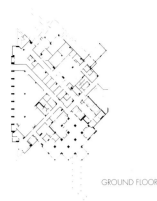

From the start, KMD's job was aided by its long history of work with Marin General. The firm implemented a triangular floor configuration, pioneered by KMD earlier at Saint Mark's Hospital in Salt Lake City. This resulted in greater economies of staffing, a shortening of travel distances, and better visibility of patient rooms. The triangular configuration also opened the design to the glassed-in lobbies at each corner, adding pleasing and therapeutic views of forested Marin hills from hospital corridors.

The programmatic view of the hospital was made more soothing to Marin County's activist planning community by the attention KMD designers paid to the addition's hillside context. An olive base, broken by a gray-green top, gave the five-story building a seemingly smaller mass, an openness and lightness giving the impression of a naturally flowing addition to the hillside setting. Actual floor-to-floor heights were reduced by the incorporation of an innovative, flat-slab structural system that eliminated deep framing members in the interior of the building.

Designed in the mode of what KMD principal Herb McLaughlin describes as "a medical Dagwood sandwich," the Marin General addition contains a vertical sandwich of seemingly disparate medical and staff utilities, the coherent and integral functioning of which are necessary for a successful modern hospital addition. The addition was viewed within the context of overall hospital master planning, allowing a number of renovations to older spaces to take place in a nonobtrusive way as medical functions moved into the new addition.

SITE

4   NORTH FACE; USE OF A DARKER BASE COLOR TO BREAK UP
     THE FACADE HELPS THE FIVE-STORY BUILDING FIT EASILY INTO
     ITS SURROUNDINGS.

5   A GREEN SHIP ON A COURSE THROUGH GREEN HILLS

6

7

8

6 WINDOW WALLS AND SKYLIGHTS OF MAIN ENTRANCE CREATE A DIRECT CONNECTION TO OUTSIDE LANDSCAPE.

7 MAIN LOBBY AND SECOND-FLOOR SURGERY WAITING ROOM; THE SKYLIGHTS AND WINDOW WALLS ENHANCE OVERALL SPATIAL SENSE.

8 SKYLIGHT OVER MAIN LOBBY

9 NEW MARIN GENERAL MAIN ENTRANCE AND ELEVATOR TOWER; DRAMATIC MASSING REFLECTS THE SLOPE OF NEARBY MARIN HILLSIDES.

9

1 CURVILINEAR FORM
SURROUNDING CUTAWAY
ON SECOND-FLOOR PATIENT
WINDOW, SOUTHWESTERN
COLORS AND FORMS

2 MAIN ENTRANCE IS THE
CURVED PIVOT OF THE
MEDICAL MALL'S TWO ARMS.

Mercy Southwest Health Campus in Bakersfield is a low-rise, 127,000-square-foot (11,430-square-meter) hospital, ambulatory care, and birthing center, and two adjacent medical office buildings. A 175-unit continuing care retirement center, medical retail center, and day-care center are planned for future development. With various medical and nonmedical functions distributed in appropriate campus structures that allowed construction costs to be minimized, Mercy Southwest is a prime example of the "medical mall" concept.

Designed, above all, for patient convenience, Mercy Southwest's diagnostic, treatment, and ancillary departments are located on the first floor with patient rooms and perinatal services on the second. The proximity of the new medical office buildings to the hospital locates physicians just steps away from their hospitalized patients. A birthing center is connected directly to doctors' offices via a bridge.

The genesis of the Southwest Health Campus began with the proposed addition of a five-story, 70,000-square-foot (6,300-square-meter) nursing tower and services building at the Mercy campus in downtown Bakersfield in 1981. In the early eighties, recognizing that the locus of medical care was shifting from inpatient to outpatient functions and that the population of the Bakersfield community was shifting to the suburbs, KMD undertook a study comparing the relative benefit of creating a new campus over expanding and renovating the old Mercy site.

The research suggested that a number of modern medical requirements could be met more efficiently by building a series of lower-cost, low-rise buildings, each with specific functions on a new campus. A selection process led to the choice of a 31-acre (12-hectare) site located in underserved and growing southwest Bakersfield.

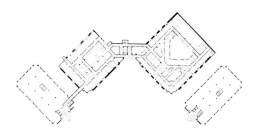

SECOND FLOOR

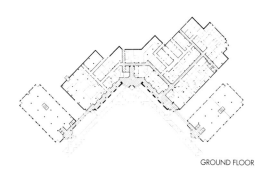

GROUND FLOOR

3

4

MERCY SOUTHWEST HEALTH CAMPUS

In collaboration with BFGC Architects, KMD designed Mercy Southwest around the concept of an open public mall. The key to this medical mall concept is a corridor running along the inside edge of the complex. The corridor connects the lobby to the wings of the hospital and then radiates out to the two medical office out-buildings. Floor-to-ceiling windows give the mall an open, airy feel and provide light to inside waiting rooms. The large, open central lobby is designed according to the KMD principle that public hospital space should provide warmth and support for anxious patients and family. The exterior is low and horizontal and finished in the earth tones matching its Southwestern locale.

Considerable sums were saved following research suggesting that the hospital norm of maintaining separate operating theaters, recovery rooms, and even nursing staffs for in- and outpatient surgery was extremely wasteful. Mercy Southwest was one of the first hospitals to combine a large number of these redundant medical functions through the design process. Further cost savings were derived from utilization of a KMD-conceived triangular floor plan for inpatient care, allowing supervision from either a central nursing station or from two substations at the apex of each triangle.

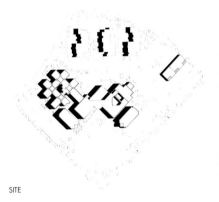

SITE

3   MEDICAL MALL; WAITING AREA ON INTERIOR CORRIDOR IS WARMLY LIT BY WINDOW WALLS.

4   THE DEEPLY RECESSED SLOT WINDOWS OF THE MAIN LOBBY FACILITATE THE ENTRY OF LIGHT WHILE SHIELDING THE SPACE FROM FIERCE SOUTHWESTERN SUNLIGHT. THE CURVE OF THE BALCONY REFLECTS THE CURVE OF MAIN ENTRY DRUM.

5   THE ENDS OF MEDICAL MALL ARE EMPHASIZED TO SIGNAL ENTRY POINTS AND HELP ALLEVIATE STRESS OF ARRIVAL.

5

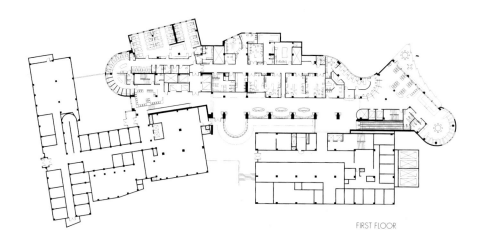

FIRST FLOOR

1 ELEVATION; THE EXTERIOR BALANCES A REASSURING
SENSE OF MODERN MEDICAL TECHNOLOGY WITH
THE HEALING ELEMENTS OF NATURAL LIGHT, OPEN
SUNNY SPACES, CURVILINEAR WINDOW WALLS,
AND SOOTHING COLORS.

CHEIL GENERAL HOSPITAL

For the last thirty years, Cheil General Hospital has been Seoul's premier center for women's care. Cheil was founded by two visionary obstetricians and gynecologists at a time when hospitals in Korea paid little attention to women's services. Today, Cheil boasts a cutting-edge in-vitro fertilization and reproductive program. Their core facility was old, small, and too limited for the tertiary level of care offered. KMD, in collaboration with SAMWOO of Korea, was retained to develop the master plan for Cheil's future expansion. Complications to the project included the need to extend the hospital to a major thoroughfare via a narrow, steep slot of adjacent land, as well as by a requirement to avoid shading a property immediately to the north. A further programmatic requirement was the need, wherever possible, to interconnect services between the existing hospital and the new expansion for convenient patient and staff flow and interaction. KMD met these difficult site constraints by creating a design that makes maximum use of the very limited building zone.

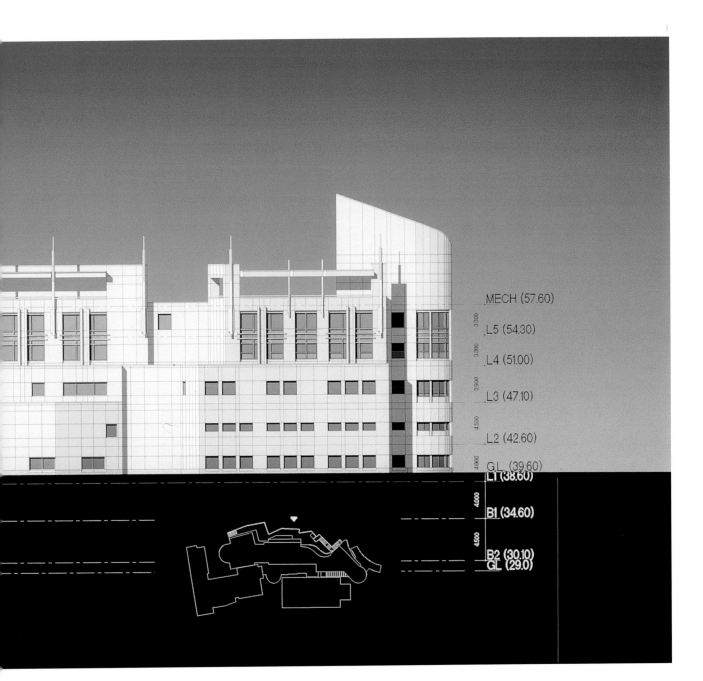

MECH (57.60)
L5 (54.30)
L4 (51.00)
L3 (47.10)
L2 (42.60)
G.L. (39.60)
L1 (38.60)
B1 (34.60)
B2 (30.10)
GL (29.0)

In KMD's design, patients arrive at Cheil's new street-level entrance and travel up a pair of escalators rising 45 feet (14 meters) to the current main entrance lobby on the hillside. The circulation gallery at this level is the hospital's major communal space. The design of this space evokes a wooded path through flora, foliage, and water. This principal floor features an ambulatory surgical suite. The floor below is designed to house an imaging department that serves inpatients and connects with existing outpatient services in an adjacent clinic building. Mezzanines are set aside for labor/delivery suites. Each of these has been planned to make the most effective use of the long, narrow site by grouping activities into clusters for efficient staffing. In obstetrics, for example, one cluster is designed for traditional labor, birthing and recovery, while another holds labor/delivery and recovery rooms designed for the new concept of family-centered care.

KMD carefully analyzed space requirements for specific surgical procedures in order to vary the sizes of operating rooms. This made it possible to increase the capacity of the hospital within the limited site constraints. Two new patient care floors feature bedrooms of contemporary western standards along with a full-term nursery for newborns. Seven levels of subterranean parking were created, employing elevators and automated parking systems to store cars below the lowest floor accessible by ramps. Because of the density of the neighborhood and very narrow streets of the city, cars may enter only at one level and leave at another, thus requiring a virtual street through the lower levels of the building.

The new main facade—seen only through a narrow gap along the downhill thoroughfare—is designed as a celebratory plaza featuring flags to draw attention of passersby, especially in winter when plants are dormant and the street trees are bare. To enliven the silhouette of the building and to allow glimpses of the hospital to be viewed from the narrow streets and alleys of the surrounding neighborhood, fan rooms have been placed at roof level.

When completed, Cheil General Hospital will not only become one of Seoul's most modern hospital facilities, it will also enable the hospital to remain in its current location and provide an enhanced physical presence to complement its reputation as one of Asia's leading hospitals.

2 EAST AND NORTH ELEVATIONS; A
   METAL SPIRE MARKS THE NEW
   OUTPATIENT ENTRANCE.

3 CHEIL'S CIRCULATION GALLERY PROVIDES
   A SENSE OF CELEBRATION AND SECURITY.

When KMD began research in 1987 for Atlanta's Grady Memorial Hospital project, the city was competing for the 1996 Olympic Games and gaining confidence in its role as a prominent international center. KMD saw that a visionary renovation and expansion of this 1,000-bed, county-funded hospital could be a key part of the realization of the new Atlanta. Grady Memorial is one of the South's largest hospitals and serves as a teaching facility for Emory University and Morehouse College medical schools.

Its tradition of collaboration allowed KMD to lead a planning and design team of thirty architects from five firms: URS Consultants Inc.; The Burlington Group; Carl Trimble Architects; Stanley, Love-Stanley P.C.; and Harrington, George and Dunn, P.C. The goal of the collaboration was to transform Grady into a forward-looking center of modern medicine. One of the initial decisions was to meet the program requirements through expansion and renovation rather than by building an entirely new hospital. This led to a 40 percent cost savings.

Following one of KMD's key themes, the team focused on the opportunity to develop a facility that would enhance treatment and foster healing. The major project components were completed in 1995, coincidental with the hospital's 100th anniversary. The project includes 700,000 square feet (63,000 square meters) of new construction and 1.2 million square feet (90,000 square meters) of renovation.

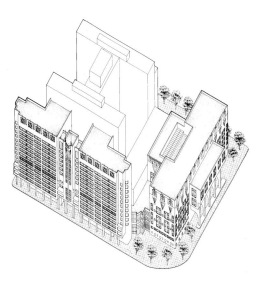

AXONOMETRIC PROJECTION

1   ARCHES FACED WITH STONE SUPPORT LARGE UPPER FLOORS OF THE
    NEW SOUTH WING.

2   PATTERNS CREATED IN THE STONE BREAK DOWN THE SCALE AND
    ADD VISUAL INTEREST TO THE SOUTH WING FACADE.

3   NEW SOUTHWING CLINIC BUILDING WITH METAL AND GLASS
    ENTRANCE FOR OUTPATIENTS

2

3

4   SKYLIGHT OVER ENTRANCE IN MAIN ATRIUM VESTIBULE

5   FACADE OF CLINIC; DIFFERENT STONES AND
       PATTERNS BREAK DOWN SCALE AND CREATE INTEREST.

KMD's experience in health-care design has led to an understanding that traffic control is a key to smooth hospital functioning. This is particularly important at Grady Memorial, one of the nation's busiest hospitals with over three million patient visits per year. To deal with traffic considerations, the design team began by relocating the emergency entrance and creating a new two-block-long entry zone along Butler Street, as well as a block-long discharge zone along Pratt Street. This reduces pedestrian/vehicle conflicts and provides convenient access points for clinics and for all departments in the hospital, which is zoned laterally by function and vertically by service.

The New South Wing consists of a ten-story, 373,000-square-foot (33,570-square-meter) diagnostic clinic and treatment center, housing units for surgery, labor and delivery, a 120-bassinet neonatal intensive care unit, 88 intensive care beds, and outpatient clinics that accommodate as many as 3,000 people per day. A new 16,000-square-foot (1,440-square-meter) service building, anchored by a relocated loading dock, connects via tunnel to the main hospital's service floor. A McDonald's provides food-service convenience on the corner of the site, adjacent to a proposed retail complex that will raise the amenity level for staff and visitors.

Renovation of the existing 1.2-million-square-foot (90,000-square-meter) main building includes infrastructure upgrades, replacement of windows for energy conservation, and construction of two stair/mechanical towers.

A   NEW SOUTH WING

B   EMERGENCY SERVICES ADDITION

C   EXPANDED INPATIENT CARE TOWERS

D   NEW OUTPATIENT IMAGING

E   NEW SERVICES BUILDING

F   ORIGINAL GRADY HOSPITAL

G   PEDIATRIC PAVILION

H   NEW PARKING GARAGE

I   HOSPITAL RENOVATION

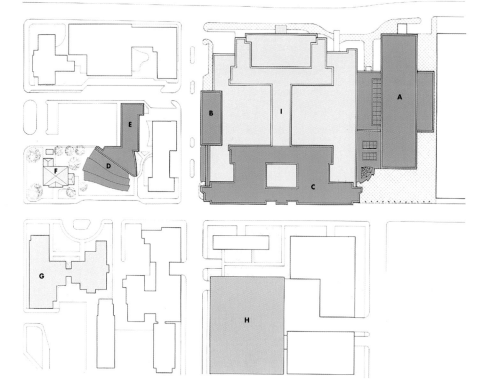

SITE

7

6 ATRIUM CREATES MAJOR CELEBRATORY CIRCULATION SPACE AND SOURCE OF NATURAL LIGHT FOR ONE OF THE NATION'S BUSIEST CLINICS.

7 RICHLY PATTERNED FLOOR IN THE ATRIUM ENLIVENS THE ENVIRONMENT.

8 ARCHWAY SIZED FOR PASSAGE OF FIRE ENGINES

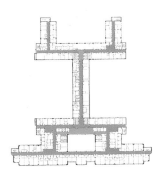

TENTH FLOOR

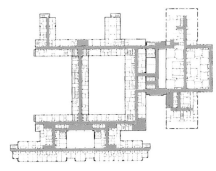

SIXTH FLOOR

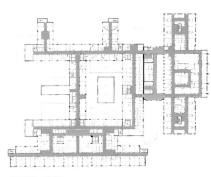

FOURTH FLOOR

THIRD FLOOR

8

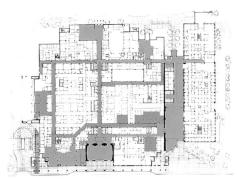

GROUND FLOOR

6

One of the most important design innovations is a fourteen-story bed tower created by "laminating" 262,000 square feet (23,600 square meters) of new construction alongside 265,000 square feet (23,900 square meters) of renovated space. This facility replaces outdated, inefficient nursing units that cost the hospital $6 million per year in internal patient transfers, with a flexible and operationally efficient tower. The new design places more than four-fifths of the hospital's adult beds into efficiently organized forty-one-bed nursing units, paired to allow the sharing of support areas and to accommodate "swing rooms" that can be a part of either adjacent unit.

10

11

9 FACING DOWNTOWN ATLANTA, GRADY'S NEW FACADE CELEBRATES AN IMPORTANT COMMUNITY FACILITY.

10 DECORATIVE ELEMENTS GIVE GRADY A DISTINCTIVE, NONINSTITUTIONAL LOOK.

11 WINDOW FROM THIRTEENTH-FLOOR PSYCHIATRIC UNIT LOOKING TOWARD DOWNTOWN ATLANTA

12 CANOPY LARGE ENOUGH TO COVER TEN AMBULANCES AT ONCE; NOTE CONTRAST OF OLD AND NEW FACADES IN BACKGROUND.

12

Each building and major entrance to Grady was designed to be identifiable as a destination within the campus building complex, while still fitting into the overall design scheme of the hospital. Thus, the image of the new south wing is related to, but different from, that of the nursing tower. The outpatient entrance and lobby of the new south wing, with its raised plaza and curved facade, differ from the arcade and main entry of the nursing tower while maintaining some elements in common.

Similarly, the 12,000-square-foot (1,080-square-meter) outpatient imaging building establishes itself as unique in character, while still embodying design elements that make it a clear member of the Grady family. Connected to the main hospital via a sky-it below-grade pedestrian link, the glass and steel imaging building reflects the high-tech nature of the processes taking place inside, while at the same time reflecting the brick and stone colors of adjacent Grady buildings.

13 LIGHT-FILLED ENTRY TO OUTPATIENT IMAGING BUILDING

14 EXTERIOR OF OUTPATIENT IMAGING BUILDING AT GRADY

15 DETAIL, ENTRANCE TO OUTPATIENT IMAGING BUILDING

HI-DESERT MEDICAL CENTER

JOSHUA TREE, CALIFORNIA

Rising from the barren desert near Joshua Tree National Monument in California, the sand-colored Hi-Desert Medical Center looks more like an old Southwest mission than a modern, skilled nursing facility. This KMD-designed healing oasis north of Palm Springs is set into a sloping hillside against a backdrop of jagged rock and mountains, coexisting with native grasses and cacti.

Located in an area with a large population of retirees, this nursing facility was financed with community taxes. KMD was commissioned to design a plan for expansion of the existing Hi-Desert Memorial Hospital as well as to design the new skilled nursing facility. Completed in 1990, the nursing facility is a one-story, 38,000-square-foot (3,420-square-meter) structure designed to accommodate 120 subacute and long-term care patients. The center, with its cleanly defined stucco walls, is designed around a central outdoor courtyard. Thanks to walls that shield it from harsh desert winds, the Hi-Desert courtyard has its own microclimate and provides respite for both patients and plant life. The building's sculptured south facade houses two simple T-shaped patient wings, with a nurse's station placed at the intersection of each wing. Each station handles sixty beds and offers clear views of the central courtyard, lounges, and patient rooms.

Other offices and functions, such as physical therapy, administration, dining area, and chapel, are placed along a patient "street" to encourage patients who are ambulatory to mingle in the building's comfortable public spaces.

On the exterior, simple architectural details maintain harmony with the natural setting. Small, recessed windows, a shaded terrace, vine-covered trellises, and a chapel tower provide a striking visual focus amid the stark desert setting.

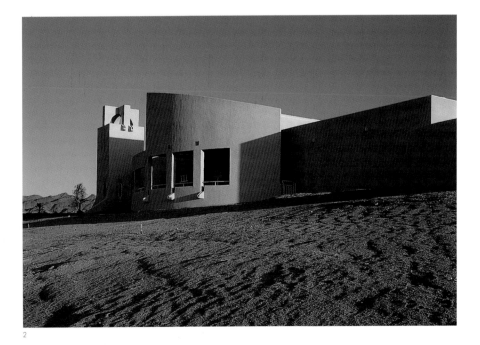

1

2

125

3

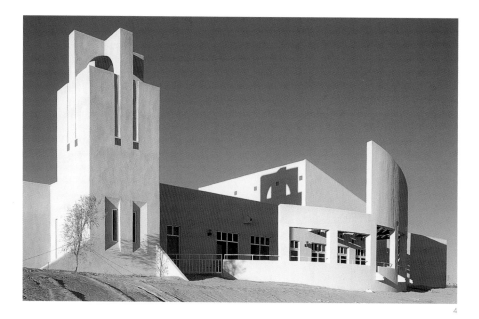

4

3 RECREATION AREA LOOKING OUT TO
  PATIENT COURTYARD

4 VERANDA OFFERS PATIENT ACCESS TO
  OUTDOORS, WITH PROTECTION FROM THE
  DESERT SUN AND WIND.

5 CLOSE UP OF FRONT FACADE; PLAY OF
  DESERT LIGHT AND SHADOW

6 THE CHAPEL TOWER PROVIDES A STRONG
  IMAGE OF SOUTHWESTERN CULTURE.

7 FORMED LIKE A SAIL, THE CURVED WALL
  SHADES AND PROTECTS THE VERANDAH.

5

6

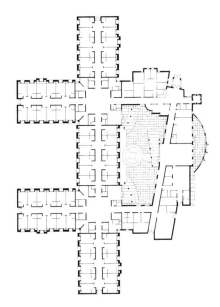

GROUND FLOOR

7

UCSD MEDICAL CENTER

SAN DIEGO, CALIFORNIA

KMD surveyed hospital patient attitudes in the 1970s and made two surprising discoveries. One is that hospital lobbies, rather than serving as waiting areas, actually function as high-traffic reception areas where people form their first impression of an institution. In addition, KMD found that patients prefer high-tech, state-of-the-art hospital treatment areas.

Accordingly, in the late 1980s KMD, along with architect of record, Neptune Thomas Davis, designed a new outpatient surgery tower for the University of California San Diego Medical Center that is both high-tech and humane. Completed in 1992, the 90,000-square-foot (8,100-square-meter), four-story facility houses units for outpatient surgery, bronchoscopy, hemodialysis, cardiology, pulmonary function, and medical records. The stucco, steel, and glass-clad structure is connected to the existing main hospital and clinic via a tower for public access to the hospital that contains new elevators as well as classrooms and offices for the University's teaching physicians and medical students. Futuristic spires reach skyward, adding a dramatic design element to the tower's exterior.

1   NEW ENTRY ROTUNDA AND TOWER; NOTE DIAGONAL
PATTERNS OF SEISMIC BRACING SYSTEM AT OLDER
HOSPITAL BUILDING.

2   FRONT VIEW OF PERFORATED ALUMINUM SUNSHADES

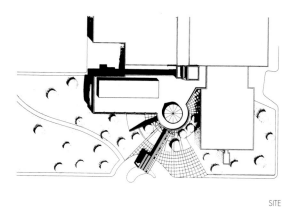

Most striking is the Center's grand entrance and lobby area. KMD moved the main hospital entrance from the north to the south side of the site, which is closer to parking structures, offers more space, and opens every floor to a view of downtown San Diego. A steel canopy extends from the lobby and stretches across the entry driveway to shelter arriving patients. A three-story, sunlit rotunda, with indoor palm trees and terrazzo floors, greets newcomers and then directs them to admissions area, gift shop, and medical units. Outside, steel mesh sunscreens shaped like curving sails shield the lobby from the intense California sun.

KMD's combination of rectangular surgery wing, cylindrical lobby, and spire-topped elevator tower offers a visual respite from the Modernist concrete-box design of the original 1962 hospital. KMD was also able to give the old building a facelift in the form of a seismic upgrade; steel "X" braces were added to form an exterior wall for stability and to emphasize a diagonal articulation. The X-pattern was continued by way of embossed stucco on the tower's west side.

3 SPIRE-TOPPED ELEVATOR TOWER OFFERS A NEW VISUAL LANDMARK FOR UCSD MEDICAL CENTER.

4 ENTRYWAY TO UCSD MEDICAL TOWER; THREE-STORY, SUNLIT ROTUNDA GREETS PATIENTS, FAMILY, AND STAFF.

5 FORTY-FIVE-FOOT-HIGH LOBBY IS FINISHED WITH TERRAZZO FLOORS AND PIERCED BY 218-FOOT-LONG, GRANITE-CLAD SCREEN WALL THAT CONTINUES ONTO THE STREET.

6 ENTRANCE ROTUNDA INTERIOR; PATTERNS OF MORNING LIGHT CREATE INTEREST.

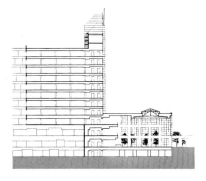

SECTION

5

6

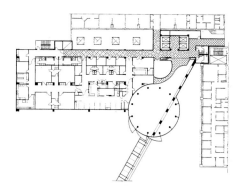

THIRD FLOOR

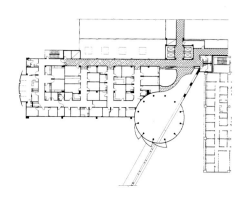

SECOND FLOOR

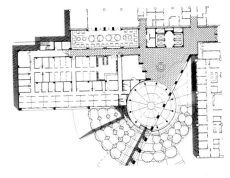

FIRST FLOOR

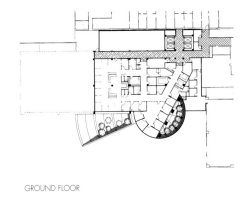

GROUND FLOOR

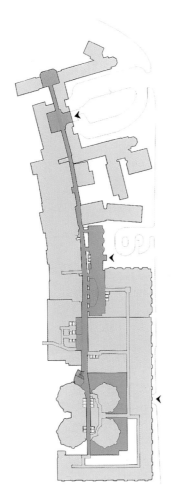

A leading teaching hospital for Harvard Medical School, Brigham & Women's Hospital in Boston is one of the region's busiest medical complexes. As it grew over the years, a jumble of new buildings were built along a rambling and intensely used corridor dubbed "The Pike," a mordant reference to the Massachusetts Turnpike at rush hour.

By the mid-1980s, the 1.1-million-square-foot (99,000-square-meter) hospital was in need of more space for outpatient services, as well as a new look. Brigham and Women's is regarded as one of the nation's leading hospitals, but there was a strong perception by staff that the quality of its architecture did not measure up to its medical status. In 1984, KMD was retained to develop a 50-year master plan for the organization, development, phased renovation, and expansion of the hospital, and for the creation of a new, modern, inviting, and sophisticated look.

Notorious though "The Pike" was, KMD immediately recognized its vast potential and urged its renovation as a central part of the overall plan. "The Pike" could become an important asset, a high-traffic thoroughfare that, with the right treatment, could be transformed into a grand "medical boulevard," acting both as a meeting place and as a central organizing "spine."

1 "THE PIKE" EXTENDS THE LENGTH OF THE CAMPUS AS A PEDESTRIAN THOROUGHFARE, CONNECTING MAJOR ENTRANCES, PUBLIC SPACES, AND VERTICAL CIRCULATION COVES.

2 INCOMING VISITORS ARE GREETED WITH A LARGE WELL-LIT INFORMATION POST.

3 ACCESS TO "THE PIKE" IS CLEARLY PRESENTED.

4 THE LOBBY BECOMES A MEETING PLACE FOR PERSONNEL AND VISITORS.

5 AN ARRAY OF MEDICAL AND VISITOR SERVICES ARE VISIBLE AND AVAILABLE IN NODES CONNECTED BY "THE PIKE."

6

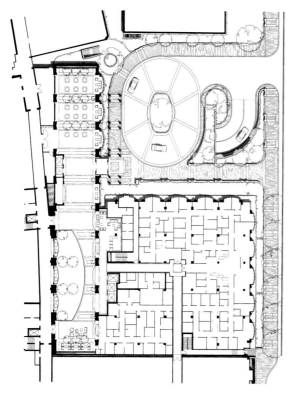

SECOND FLOOR

KMD's proposed renovation of "The Pike" was part of the overall plan to provide an additional million square feet of expansion, the first phase of which would include a centrally located, four-story ambulatory services facility. This ambulatory service building was designed with four floors housing outpatient services generating two hundred thousand visits per year. These include offices for hospital-based and private physicians' groups, including dental and surgical groups. Also included are floors containing radiology units, physical and occupational therapy, a blood bank, and a parking garage.

The building's multilevel atrium lobby was designed to create a new entry to the hospital campus, as well as comfortable, skylit waiting and conference areas. The color scheme inside and out contains soft hues to make the interior calming and the exterior unimposing. Planters filled with trees and greenery bring the healing touch of nature into the hospital.

8

9

10

Recognizing the hospital's site in a greater Boston residential neighborhood filled with triple-decker row houses, the outpatient clinic's street-side facade consists of three-story curved bays, which complement the architectural style and height of Boston's residential architecture.

The ambulatory care building was undertaken by KMD, with Tsoi Kobus Architects as Associate Architect. On two subsequent projects KMD served as design and planning consultant to TKA. The 125,000-square-foot (11,250-square-meter) Center for Women and Newborns, completed in 1994, and the renovation and expansion of the main tower lobby are both extensions of "The Pike" concept. Today, KMD continues to work with Brigham and Women's on several additional projects and to assist in its partnership with Massachusetts General Hospital.

8-10 USE OF A UNIQUE DESIGN VOCABULARY REDUCES THE ANXIETY OF THE ARRIVING PATIENT DURING RECEPTION AND REGISTRATION.

11 THE BUILDING SERVES AS AN ICON FOR THE CENTER FOR WOMEN AND NEWBORNS AND REINFORCES THE RESIDENTIAL IMAGERY OF THE CAMPUS.

12 THE PIKE; A "MEDICAL BOULEVARD" PROVIDES CONTINUITY AND ORIENTATION THROUGH THE LARGE MEDICAL COMPLEX.

13 THE AMBULATORY CARE BUILDING COMPLEMENTS THE FORM AND SCALE OF THE SURROUNDING NEIGHBORHOOD TOWNHOUSES.

11

12

13

Completed in 1992 for United Health Services, the Decker Center for Advanced Medical Treatment was the product of a fundamental change in health care in the Tri-Cities upstate New York area of Binghamton, Johnson City, and Ideal. With three hospitals merging to form United Health Services, the viability of the system depended on a focused, low-cost, inviting, and patient-responsive program. The Decker Center, the Senior Living Center, and the Community Hospital were the tremendously successful result of a community and health care system collaboration.

KMD's Long Range Facilities Development Plan relied on the achievement of a community consensus, uniting three historically diverse care constituencies. KMD initiated a research program to find common ground that would allow hospital assets to be most efficiently managed.

KMD's process of inquiry and research helped achieve consensus and led to the completion of a plan to maintain all three facilities through increased specialization, increased outpatient care, downsizing the number of inpatient beds, and advancing the technology for intensive care. Suburban Ideal Hospital, the smallest of the three, was converted into a senior living center. The Binghamton General Hospital was transformed into a smaller 253-bed community teaching hospital that included new outpatient care services, a family health center, psychiatric nursing and intensive care units.

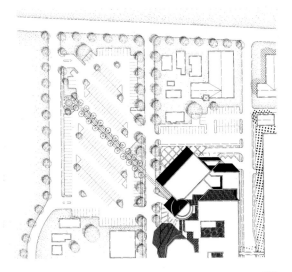

SITE

DECKER CENTER FOR ADVANCED MEDICAL TREATMENT

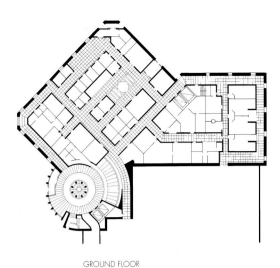

The centerpiece of the UHS project is the new Decker Center for Advanced Medical Treatment at the Wilson Memorial Regional Medical Center in Johnson City. Designed to create a cost-effective and patient-responsive facility, the Decker Center's 87,000-square-foot (7,830-square-meter) facility serves both outpatients entering the health care system and intensively ill or injured patients by making high technology, surgical, imaging, and emergency services available to both.

The design of the facility reflects the medical sophistication and efficiency of the institution and its staff, as well as the supportive richness of the community traditions. This is evident in the intricately patterned brick extensions with special accents and ornate metal grillwork.

Recalling the many local church towers around the hospital, the elevator tower and an airy rotunda act as reassuring icons of community for patients and families. A simple, direct, and recognizable circulation system provides a comfortable and effective floor plan so that patients can conveniently find their way to and from treatment areas in the hospital.

Designed in collaboration with the DeWolff Partnership of Rochester, New York, and the Burlington Group of Burlington, Massachusetts, UHS achieved its successful recombination through the maximal reuse of the existing facilities based on the level of obsolescence and appropriate configuration. The architecture created valuable environmental benefits and support for the healing process.

2   INTRICATE GRILL AND BRICKWORK BRING A SENSE
    OF HUMAN SCALE TO THIS LARGE COMPLEX.

3   EAST ELEVATION; ELEGANT, ECONOMICAL
    DESIGN DETAILS IN METAL AND BRICK; OLD BUILDING
    MATERIALS/CONTEMPORARY LOOK

4   WINDOWS ARE CELEBRATED IN THIS OFTEN COLD
    ENVIRONMENT.

5   THE OVERALL COMPLEX PRESENTS A RICH, HIGHLY
    TEXTURED YET UNITED IMAGE.

6   ARCHITECTURAL MATERIALS AND DETAILS COMPLIMENT
    EXISTING, REGIONAL DESIGN.

6

In the early 1980s, professionals at the California Medical Center recognized that they had outgrown their original 1964 facility. Floor area was too small for effective remodeling, and a physical plant designed for an inpatient population was not appropriate to a market with increasing requirements for more comprehensive diagnosis and both inpatient and outpatient treatment facilities.

The hospital developed plans to replace many of the its major diagnostic treatment and service departments and to replace or upgrade 344 acute-care beds. Beyond the programmatic requirements, KMD designers faced a constricted site and the constraints of rigorous development regulations.

The firm devised an innovative plan that integrated an existing inpatient care wing with a new addition, forming T-shaped nursing units on six upper levels and integrating new diagnostic facilities for the inpatient and outpatient population at the lower levels. A vertical circulation core—forming the attachment to a large new triangular tower resembling an "arrowhead"—serves the link. The attachment of the triangle to the elevator core along the hypotenuse opens the apexes for the creation of waiting room/solariums with striking views of the Los Angeles skyline to the north, as well as landscaped areas of the campus. Within the zone of contact between the old and new buildings is a lush courtyard that captures the morning sun but remains shaded during hot afternoons. The main lobby and principal linking corridor at grade both face the court.

This awareness of the outdoors is shared by inpatients as well. All beds are placed so that patients have views both out of the window and into the corridors. A diamond-shaped, two-bed patient room is bounded by a pair of single care rooms, in an arrangement developed through the use of full-scale mock-ups to determine the most efficient placement and movement of people and equipment within rooms that meet state-prescribed maximum areas. The structural systems to resist seismic forces resulted in deep overhangs that shield the strong Los Angeles sun but allow generous window sizes to provide excellent views for the patients.

The limited site called for the stacking of services that carried very different functional requirements and size. The tapering floors of the new tower consist of a birthing floor, surgery, critical care, central processing, and a ground floor with a lobby and cafeteria.

The cafeteria, lobby, and an octagonal admitting pavilion define a new entry court, public plaza, and entry drive for the use of patients, employees, and the public. With the arrowhead tower, they give the hospital new visibility and enhanced presence in the Los Angeles community.

2

3

1 SIZE AND SCALE BALANCE IN THE CREATION OF
   OPEN SPACE WITHIN THE LARGE BUILDINGS AND
   INTENSELY DEVELOPED COMPLEX.

2 THE ORIGINAL HOSPITAL BUILDING WAS ELEGANT,
   BUT INADEQUATE FOR CURRENT HEALTH-CARE
   REQUIREMENTS.

3 THE NEW PATIENT CARE WING RESPECTS THE
   CONTEXT OF THE MEDICAL CAMPUS WHILE ESTAB-
   LISHING A MORE MODERN PRESENCE.

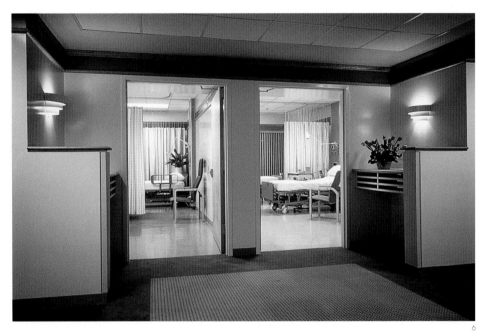

4   THE NEW CAFETERIA WAS DESIGNED TO BE
     COMFORTABLE AND RELAXING.

5   NURSES' STATIONS FEATURE CLEAR SIGHT LINES TO KEY
     PATIENT AREAS.

6   THE FLOOR PLAN AND PATIENT ROOM LAYOUTS
     PROVIDE AREAS FOR EQUIPMENT STORAGE AND STAGING.

7   PATIENT ROOMS MAINTAIN PRIVACY WHILE ALLOWING FOR
     GOOD SIGHT SUPERVISION FROM THE NURSES' STATION.

8   GENTLE CURVES MAKE THE USUALLY TIRESOME CHORE OF
     WALKING FROM ONE WING TO THE OTHER A PLEASANT,
     LIGHT-FILLED EXPERIENCE.

9   INTERIOR CORRIDOR LOOKS OUT ON LANDSCAPED
     COURTYARD, PROVIDING A SUN-FILLED RETREAT FROM THE
     INTENSITY OF LIFE IN A LARGE HOSPITAL.

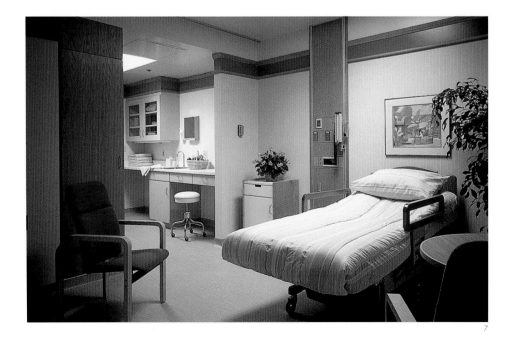

TYPICAL FLOOR

FIFTH FLOOR

FOURTH FLOOR

THIRD FLOOR

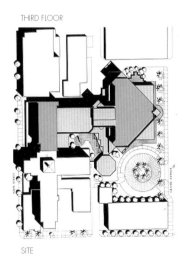

SITE

Dominating the Seattle skyline from a location on a high bluff over-looking downtown, the Harborview Medical Center is an historic landmark as well as one of the premier medical facilities in the northwestern United States. Harborview serves not only as the King County public hospital and teaching facility for the University of Washington, but also as the officially designated Trauma Center for the Northwest Region, with a reach extending as far north and east as Alaska and Montana.

KMD's plan for the $104 million Harborview renovation and addition project addressed the key issues of strict space constraints and the need to minimize disruption during construction. Completed in January 1997, the project provides two six-story pavilions covering four city blocks, for inpatient and ambulatory care, as well as a 162,000-square-foot (14,580-square-meter) renovation that expands or replaces all major diagnostic and treatment departments. KMD's innovative response met Harborview's program goals under budget—and in 20 percent less volume—through planning efficiencies and functional reorganizations. The merger of the trauma and radiology programs creates a new rapid-response center that will reduce mortality and maximize staff efficiency. The design also restores one of Seattle's most prominent facades to a style complimentary to its original 1920s Art Deco and Neo-Gothic roots.

1

2

1   THE NEW IMAGE OF THE HOSPITAL PRESENTS A MORE INTRICATE, EXCITING CONTEXTUAL FACADE TO THE CITY BELOW.

2   NEW ENTRY UNITES TWO NEW WINGS AND SERVES AS A MAJOR ORGANIZING ELEMENT.

3   ETCHED ARTGLASS SEPARATES THE LOBBY FROM THE SKYLIGHT-COVERED CAFETERIA.

4   ORGANIC FORMS, ARTWORK, AND COLOR ARE USED IN THE CAFETERIA TO CREATE
    A PEACEFUL REFUGE FROM THE STRESSFUL ENVIRONMENT OF THE TRAUMA CENTER.

5   TWO PRIMARY ENTRANCES AT DIFFERENT LEVELS ARE LINKED THROUGH CREATION
    OF AN AGORA WITH A GRAND STAIR AS THE CENTERPIECE.

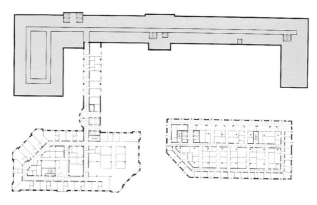

FOURTH FLOOR

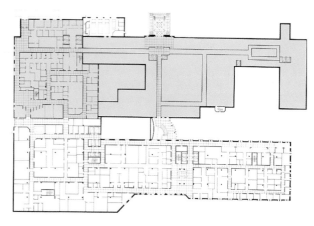

FIRST FLOOR

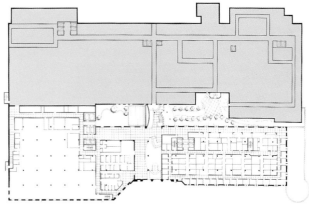

GROUND FLOOR

In its initial conception, KMD created two buildings that separated trauma center beds from ambulatory care clinics. The plan not only simplified complex medical functions into understandable elements, but also enabled the creation of a new civic image for Harborview through the design of a clearly visible entry more sympathetic to the hospital's original design than the two indifferently designed modernist wings completed earlier. The new construction is sheathed in brick laid in patterns evocative of the original hospital design elements. The two pavilion facades differ subtly, each incorporating elements that reflect the uses within: patient rooms in one and examination rooms, offices, and waiting areas in the other.

The inpatient care tower consists of a new three-story Trauma Center topped by four floors of beds for critical care, acute care, psychiatry, rehabilitation and a special unit for epileptic patients. The lower levels accommodate the horizontal extension of emergency and surgery units, as well as the relocation of laboratory and imaging facilities. This allowed for the differentiation of the emergency unit between these zones for major and minor trauma as well as urgent walk-in traffic. The trauma tower is attached to the older hospital at every inpatient care level. This allows the efficiency of only one new elevator core to serve all inpatient needs. Public elevator lobbies feature outside views and access to rooftops, many landscaped with sitting and strolling areas that offer outstanding views of the city center and harbor below.

5

6

7

8

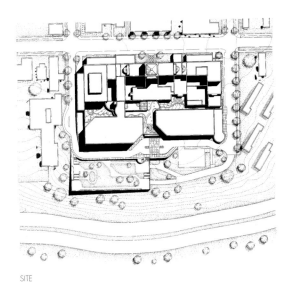

SITE

6   THE CANOPY AT THE MAIN ENTRANCE PROVIDES
    SHELTER FOR LOADING VEHICLES.

7   THE SKYLINE DOMINANCE OF THE 1929 TOWER IS
    REINFORCED THROUGH A CONTEXTUAL DESIGN
    WHICH CREATES TWO FLANKING WINGS
    SEPARATED BY THE NEW ENTRANCE AND LOBBY.

8   THE DESIGN AND DETAILING CELEBRATE THIS
    ARCHITECTURAL LANDMARK AND CONTRAST WITH
    THE GLASS TOWERS OF THE FINANCIAL CORE.

SUTTER MATERNITY AND SURGERY CENTER

SANTA CRUZ, CALIFORNIA

A sunny plaza, a magnificent oak tree, and a Mediterranean-toned facade welcome patients, families, and staff to the Sutter Maternity and Surgery Center of Santa Cruz. The center provides family-centered care, featuring birthing services and inpatient/outpatient surgery and recovery. Located at the northern edge of the scenic Monterey Bay, the center's design complements the region's natural surroundings and temperate climate while addressing the health-care needs of Santa Cruz. The noninstitutional design conveys a human scale and sense of well-being in a homelike environment.

The two-story, 65,000-square-foot (5,850-square-meter) facility is situated on 3.8 acres (1.5 hectares), adjacent to two affiliated medical office buildings. By preserving a number of existing mature trees, the facility illustrates a strong sense of balance with the natural elements. A dramatic visual effect occurs as the sunlight moves over the facade, drawing attention to the subtle design of the building. The articulated elements of the rounded roof structures and second-story patient room terraces create the perception of a residential structure. The trellis's shadow washes the entrance with distinctive light patterns and serves to identify the main entrance of the center. Detailed window mullions, employed throughout the design, provide the overall facade with rhythm and continuity. The entry opens to a two-story rotunda which is bathed in sunlight. Five bays of double-height glazing allow light to create a joyous space.

The surgery center, orthopedic clinic, surgery nursing unit, and birthing center are entered directly from the rotunda. The surgery center occupies half of the first floor with additional spaces programmed for the orthopedic clinic, radiology, and support services. The second floor south wing includes a birthing center featuring twelve LDRP suites. An eighteen-bed surgical nursing unit occupies the north wing of the second floor accommodating limited patient stays, few of which exceed three days. Gentle arched ceilings and muted interiors throughout the facility create a calm and comforting atmosphere.

The experience of visiting the center provides one with a feeling of transition. Conventional perceptions of a hospital give way to a new vision and understanding of today's health-care environment. The center literally provides a gateway to a new era of health-care delivery for the local community. The innovative integration of the setting, architecture, and care giving creates the foundation for a new perception of health-care design and architecture.

1 THE GLOW OF THE ROTUNDA AT SUNSET IS A WELCOMING BEACON TO PATIENTS AND VISITORS.

2 BIRTHING AND SURGICAL RECOVERY SUITES ARE ORGANIZED ALONG EIGHTEEN-FOOT-WIDE CORRIDORS. EACH ARCHED CORRIDOR IS PUNCTUATED BY SKYLIGHTS; FAMILY WAITING AREAS RELATE TO FAUX-FIREPLACES BETWEEN PATIENT BEDROOM DOORS.

3 THE TWO-STORY ROTUNDA CLEARLY EXPRESSES THE BUILDING'S ENTRANCE AND THE CENTRALITY OF THE PLAN BEYOND. HAVING ARRIVED AT THE SECOND FLOOR BY STAIR OR ELEVATOR, THE PATIENT AND FAMILY LOOK THROUGH FLOOR-TO-CEILING WINDOWS TO A PARK-LIKE SETTING.

4 SPACIOUS LDRP SUITES ARE FUNCTIONALLY ZONED TO ACCOMMODATE THE NEEDS OF THE STAFF AND THE FAMILY. FRENCH DOORS OPEN ONTO EXTERIOR BALCONIES PROVIDING A PRIVATE OUTDOOR RETREAT FOR FAMILY MEMBERS.

5

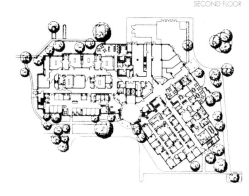

6

7

5   ROOF FORMS, OPEN TRELLISES, AND BALCONIES GIVE VISUAL AND
    SPATIAL TEXTURE.

6   BUILDING IS SITED TO CREATE A SMALL PARK WITH THE ENTRANCE
    ROTUNDA SERVING TO UNITE THE BUILDING'S TWO WINGS.

7   A GROVE OF REDWOODS AND HERITAGE OAKS CASTS BOLD
    SHADOWS ON THE FRONT FACADE ALL AFTERNOON.

8   THE RHYTHM OF THE UPPER FLOORS IS SET BY ALTERNATING PAIRS OF
    PATIENT ROOM WINDOWS AND RECESSED BALCONIES.

8

TWO RODEO DRIVE

A nostalgic, hand-carved Italian granite fountain murmuring at Two Rodeo Drive in Beverly Hills. A splash of neon announcing that San Diego's Price Center cafe is open for cappuccino at midnight. The towering, transparent glass cubes of San Francisco's Galaxy Theater glowing seductively in the pre-movie twilight of dusk.

These are the beckoning symbols of effective placemaking design and of skillfully rendered details that mark the scope of KMD's highly successful retail projects.

Moving beyond the prosaic cookie-cutter approach that characterizes the "malling" of the American sub-urbs, KMD has taken its Urban Agora concept and utilized it to transform retail into something as entertaining as it is commercial. But unlike the strategic strike shopping that has come to characterize mall retail, a key element shared by all of KMD's retail projects is that they are places so infused with energy, variety, and change, that repeat visits become the norm rather than the exception.

Successes have been notable. KMD's entertaining retail has achieved high lease rates and unprecedented retail sales. And it has done so in projects as diverse as the ultrachic retail Two Rodeo, the ultrabusy Price Center student union shops at UC San Diego, and the village-within-a-village of One Colorado Boulevard, a project that is in part responsible for the revitalization of "Old Pasadena."

Drawing upon lessons learned in a variety of placemaking venues, KMD helped spearhead the Urban Entertainment concept that is reshaping and re-energizing shopping in the 1990s. This trend coincided with the fact that as the "Malling of America" reached its peak, planners, urbanists and shoppers themselves began to recognize that a certain vitality and interaction was missing from the experience.

What was absent was a raw energy often found in city streets and town squares with their mix of retail, entertainment, restaurant, and service providers. With its experiences in urban design and commitment to placemaking, KMD began to take a leadership position in a design and marketing strategy that sought to reinvent the urban experience within the convenience, safety, and vitality of a planned environment. By employing insights gained through research and practice, this placemaking retail, often utilizing entertainment features as a catalyst, began to successfully transform the way people shopped, interacted, and used retail centers.

More, these centers work for users and owners alike: According to the *New York Times'* Paul Goldberger, Two Rodeo Drive gave Los Angeles something it had lacked: a pedestrian shopping street, Via Rodeo. One Colorado is serving as a catalyst to the revitalization of Old Pasadena, while the Price Center reinterprets the heart of a campus and puts the "there" in UC San Diego.

PRICE CENTER

And though the planning is contemporary, KMD is not averse to drawing from historicist themes or stage-set approaches to create the type of experiences that both compliment and complete the urban entertainment equation. Exteriors, exemplified by the eerily authentic European shopping street of Two Rodeo Drive or the Hollywood retrographics of Citiwalk Phase II, are designed as landmark destinations. Rich, highly-charged architectural detail foreshadows the high fashion, high-Hollywood or high sales volume experience awaiting within and helps draw strollers inside.

People, naturally, play a central role in KMD's entertaining retail concept, showcased as vital and continuously changing sources of interest and activity in their own right. By designing areas designated for organized or spontaneous "divertissements," shoppers are transformed into participants in exciting tableaux.

The lessons of placemaking illustrate that the Urban Entertainment Center should be enlivened at the edges by visible activity that takes place on more than one level. People respond to light and movement—as well as detail and color—so a highly charged environment is also a highly detailed one. Moving water is also used to animate and provide a sense of activity even during low-traffic periods. Ample, comfortable, public seating in a variety of forms and configurations, encourages people to stop, congregate, and interact. Instead of feeling like shoppers hustled through a freeway-like mall, they become players on stage in their own celebratory drama. Trellises, nooks, landscaping, and secondary spaces provide scale and shelter without separating people from the activity.

GALAXY THEATER

High-quality food service also plays an important part in creating the overall experience of the Urban Entertainment Center. Restaurant seating is designed so that it is dramatically visible to and interactive with strollers, rather than being tucked away in windowless cul-de-sacs, as is often the case in malls.

But even in KMD's fanciest flights of Two Rodeo rococo and Galaxy Theater theatrics, there is a fundamental concept of intensely detailed placemaking and celebratory style. The equation is a simple one: Innovative retail concept equals commercial appeal equals greater generated income equals increased value equals higher leases. In undertaking projects like Two Rodeo and the Price Center, KMD distinguishes client needs and begins by identifying a market for their unique product before any and all design work is undertaken.

ONE COLORADO

At Two Rodeo, for example, the need to maximize street-level retail in one of the most expensive locations on the planet, led to the unique concept for a second ground floor, a shopping street over the top of actual street level. This new level is accessed by a new pedestrian street, Via Rodeo, which rises gently to an apex marked by a historical tower that serves as the pedestrian access to exit from the underground garage. This makes the visitor's initial passage a gentle downhill slope past unique shops and restaurants.

At One Colorado in Pasadena, KMD gave careful thought to bringing customers into the center of a little-trafficked downtown block. The solution included colorful destination-announcing signage, outdoor cafes and a multiplex cinema tucked below the central plaza. And for Price Center, the wants and needs of Southern California college students were minutely dissected before a single shelf was designed for what has become the most financially successful per-square-foot student union store in America.

The KMD new generation retail bottom line? The retail experience needs to be infused with an atmosphere of energy, variety, and change at the same time it maintains a sense of heritage, community, and, of course, place. But only after the economic, traffic, and market realities are studied and understood are designers set loose to create a visceral atmosphere of entertainment-oriented retail that is at its heart a smart commercial machine.

Two Rodeo Drive has been singled out by *New York Times* architectural critic Paul Goldberger as a "theme park for rich adults," and characterized by KMD principal designer Herb McLaughlin as an example of "great set design." In truth, the 107,000-square-foot (9,630-square-meter) retail complex located at the nexus of Rodeo Drive and Wilshire Boulevard in Beverly Hills is both those things—making it the ideal retail setting for a community where set design is a celebrated and highly prized art.

Two Rodeo Drive is also a highly original and profitable example of KMD's ability to "think like a developer." By moving beyond a conventional "single-box" solution, the site's value was virtually doubled with the execution of a new second level European-style shopping street that ambles through the middle of the site and yields two retail ground floors, rather than one—maximizing the amount of highly prized ground-level shopping square-footage available at one of Beverly Hills' most visible and valuable retail corners.

The solution is a finely grained shopping alley with elements of London's Bond Street, San Francisco's Maiden Lane, and Rome's Via Veneto. As Goldberger noted, Two Rodeo provides Los Angeles with something it sorely lacks: a truly pedestrian experience.

Via Rodeo, as it is called, is not only Beverly Hills' first new shopping street in decades, it is also an elegant, well-thought-out, one-of-a-kind pedestrian thorough-fare. A rich array of spaces includes highly individual limestone and brick-clad shops, a four-story tower, campanile, and grand staircases. By sloping Via Rodeo on a gentle sweep, the design creates two vital first-floor retail levels, one facing Rodeo Drive and the other, above it, fronting Via Rodeo. And, the curvature of the street creates a sense of surprise and adventure as each step reveals a new visual treat.

1   SULKA AT TWO RODEO; ITALIANATE DETAIL, AMERICAN PALETTE

2   FINE DETAILING, DOWN TO STREET SIGNS AND LIGHT STANDARDS, GIVES THIS URBAN PLACE A HIGH DEGREE OF PERSONALITY.

3   SMALL DETAILS DEFINE A PLACE, ARCHITECTURE ORCHESTRATES THE MOVEMENT OF PEOPLE IN A REVELATORY AND CELEBRATORY WAY.

4   5   6

TWO RODEO DRIVE

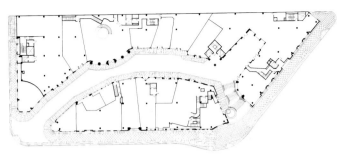

GROUND FLOOR

Along Two Rodeo's bottom level street-front, KMD incorporated more traditional retail frontage for anchor tenants including Valentino and Tiffany, flanked by grand entryways that draw pedestrians up onto Via Rodeo. Playing to Los Angeles' favored mode of transportation, an elegant arrival "plaza" was fashioned for Two Rodeo's below-ground parking garages. Shoppers are conveyed via elevator to an elegant lobby at the crest of Via Rodeo. So successful is the traffic flow into the garage and up to the second level that Tiffany's decided to rethink its merchandising layout, placing featured items on the Via Rodeo level rather than on the street level, showing the success in creating a new, urban destination.

9

7   8

4   STROLLING, SHOPPING, AND DINING ARE ALL ACCOMMODATED
     ON VIA RODEO

5   POPULAR RESTAURANTS SERVE AS ANCHORS TO THE NEW
     SHOPPING STREET.

6   A RICH AND VARIED FACADE FACES RODEO DRIVE.

7   THE CAMPANILE AT THE CORNER OF RODEO DRIVE AND VIA
     RODEO CREATES AN URBAN ICON AND THE DETAILED FACADE
     CREATES A TEXTURE OF ROMANCE AND DIVERSITY.

8   EACH TENANT APPEARS TO HAVE ITS OWN BUILDING.

9   LIGHTING, FOUNTAINS, AND COMFORTING DETAILS COMPLETE
     THE PEDESTRIAN EXPERIENCE.

This notion of destination is reinforced by historicist balconies, romantic alcoves, and whimsical columns that go beyond the clever, but often tacky, "malling" that characterizes many attempts at retail "set design." A rich composite of individual design details creates the feeling of a street in an ancient European city. Materials both rich and real complete the feeling of history and substance. These range from hand-carved fountains and gold leaf lettering to landmark lampposts and cast bronze awning brackets. The overall effect is to create a texture, diversity, and even a sense of history for a space that has quickly become distinguished as true placemaking. Two Rodeo's realization has led to the highest form of flattery: imitation in projects like the Forum Shops in Las Vegas.

10 DOWN VIA RODEO, A NOUVEAU
    CORINTHIAN TERRA-COTTA COLUMN
    AND OUTSIDE BALCONY LEAD TOWARD
    A RICH ARCHITECTURE OF IDIOSYNCRATIC,
    PERSONALIZING DETAIL. URBAN
    PLACEMAKING AT ITS MOST EFFECTIVE

11 THE TRADITION OF WATER UTILIZED AS
    A METAPHOR FOR CENTRAL URBAN
    GATHERING PLACES

12 THE SENSUAL HANDRAIL

13 DETAIL OF HAND-CARVED GRANITE
    WATER TABLE

14 FINE DETAIL IN A CAST BRONZE
    AWNING BRACKET

12

13

11

14

PRICE CENTER

Enhancing the vitality of interaction on a commuter campus, providing a focal point for student activities, and creating a thriving retail environment were goals successfully met in the design of the 164,000-square-foot (15,185-square-meter) Price Center. Completed in 1990, Price Center has quickly become the vital heart of the UCSD campus, a trend-setting retail success story and one of the highest grossing campus retail centers in the country.

An existing relation with UCSD allowed KMD to help refine the program, which began merely with a list of interior spaces to be incorporated into a single building. Starting from the premise that American campuses are too spread out and undefined, design architect KMD and associate architect, The Austin Hanson Group, focused on communal outdoor space as the key to creating the warmth and sense of community necessary to make the Price Center successful.

The actual design "broke the box" by creating two buildings, rather than a single, out-of-scale building. By spacing the Price Center's two halves around one of the main campus thoroughfares, active circulation through the complex was guaranteed and an urban piazza created.

Both Price Center buildings are faced in Jerusalem stone and Portuguese marble and are highlighted with metal grillwork. Key to creating continual circulation between indoor and outdoor spaces, the buildings are lit by window walls that open the interiors out onto the Price Center's main celebratory piazza. Garage-type roll-up doors provide a means for creating an easy flow from indoor to outdoor space in the food court area. A five-hundred-seat theater, pub, and game rooms are located in the two-story structure, while the three-story building holds a food court, a 12,000-square-foot (1,111-square-meter) ballroom, the university bookstore, and offices for student organizations.

The Price Center is the first student center in the United States designed for a mall-like commercial lease arrangement and contains six fast-food restaurants, automatic teller machine, travel agency, and cafes where students can find cappuccino, and each other, at almost any hour.

And for those who would rather watch than participate in the mix-master of social interaction that has been a Price Center constant since the day the union opened, a balcony walkway surrounding and overlooking the lower piazza was an integral part of the design, providing a place from which to observe without being compelled to enter into the action below. Well received from the start, the balcony has been given the affectionate name "Nerd's Walk," the perfect respite for the shy and retiring who none the less do not want to be left out of the action!

1 GARAGE-TYPE ROLL-UP DOORS AND DISTINCT AWNINGS PROVIDE AN EASY FLOW FROM INSIDE TO OUT AND HELP DEFINE THE RETAIL "EDGE" OF THE PIAZZA.

2 THE SENSE OF COMMUNITY IS CELEBRATED IN THE ACTIVE PIAZZA.

3 DRAMATIC LIGHTING AND WATER FEATURES PROVIDE A CAMPUS FOCUS AND HELP ADD DRAMA TO THE PIAZZA.

4   NEON-ACCENTED CONFERENCE ROOM AREA
    ENTRANCE AT TOP OF STAIRS FROM PIAZZA

5   INTERIOR STREET COMBINES LOUNGE AREAS WITH
    A PASSAGEWAY CREATING COLLEGIAL, INFORMAL
    MEETING PLACES.

6   AFTERNOON AT THE PRICE CENTER;
    STAIRS CONNECT PLAZA LEVEL AND NERD'S WALK.

5

4

6

7   THE STRONG GEOMETRY OF BUILDING EDGES
        HELPS DEFINE BOTH INTERIOR AND EXTERIOR SPACE
        AND SERVES TO CREATE A SENSE OF EXCITEMENT
        FOR USERS WITHIN.

8   BY BRINGING TOGETHER STUDENT SERVICES,
        SOCIAL AND COMMERCIAL ACTIVITIES, THE COM-
        PLEX ACTS AS THE CAMPUS TOWN SQUARE.

9   THE BOOKSTORE FEATURES A "GRAND" CENTRAL
        STAIRCASE THAT UNITES ITS TWO RETAIL LEVELS.

10 MIMICKING WINDOW DETAILS IN DOWNSPOUTS
    CREATES VISUAL CONTINUITY AND COMPLEXITY
    FOR LIMITED DOLLARS.

11 EXTERIOR DECORATION USED AS COST EFFICIENT
    WAY TO EMPHASIZE THE BUILDING AS BILLBOARD

12 TRELLIS AND WINDOW DETAILING HELP GIVE
    HUMANIZING SCALE TO A LARGE BUILDING.

13 THE DRAMATIC OCULUS WINDOW WITH
    DECORATIVE GRILLWORK FACES THE VEHICULAR
    ENTRANCE AND ILLUSTRATES THE USE OF DETAIL
    AS BEACON.

10

11

12

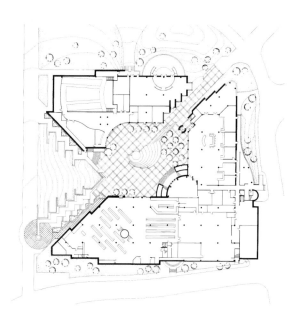

GROUND FLOOR

13

14

15

16

17

18

14   INTERIOR OF FOOD COURT

15   SECOND LEVEL CIRCULATION LEADS PAST STUDENT OFFICES.

16   CAFE AND OUTSIDE PUBLIC SPACES DURING THE DAY

17   THE CONFERENCE AREA IS POPULAR WITH OFF-CAMPUS GROUPS.

18   CURVED GLASS, LIGHTING, AND NEON CREATE A WARM, INVITING SPACE. A LIGHTED SPACE LIKE THIS NEEDS NO SIGN TO CREATE A STRONG WELCOME.

1   GALAXY THEATER AT DUSK: BUILDING AS BILLBOARD,
    A LANDMARK IN GLASS AND LIGHT

2   A HIGHLY ACTIVATED FRONTAGE PROVIDES DRAMA
    AND A SENSE OF MOVIE MAGIC AT STREET LEVEL.

Since its completion in 1984, the glowing 75-foot (23-meter) cubed-glass-and-steel tower announcing the United Artists Galaxy Theater on San Francisco's Van Ness Avenue has been one of the most identifiable symbols of the last decade's renaissance of the movie house as destination. KMD's award-winning design for the 24,000-square-foot (2,160-square-meter), four-plex Galaxy is also cited as one of the starting places for the 1990s entertainment revolution that has drawn the American public out of VCR-equipped living rooms into the exciting theater spaces that celebrate Hollywood's renewed allure.

Dramatically lit and reflecting San Francisco's early evening sky, the Galaxy tower functions as a permanent opening-night spotlight hearkening more to the glamorous palaces of the motion picture-crazy 1930s and 1940s than to the prosaic, cinder block shopping mall complexes that lent so little electricity to moviegoing from the 1960s through 1980s. Beginning with the maxim that the Galaxy's lobby would be a place where the excitement and fantasy of Hollywood would be evoked, KMD also identified other important elements in the motion picture experience. With 95 percent of a patron's time spent inside the auditorium, attention was paid to critical details of moviegoing: large screens, comfortable seats, multichannel sound systems, and excellent acoustics.

The design of the Galaxy proclaims the movie theater itself as marquee. The Galaxy design has also served a pivotal role in helping to transform one of San Francisco's major arteries from its historic role as "Auto Row" into an important regional entertainment zone. At the same time the theater's design pays textural tribute to the ornate 1920s auto showrooms that were historically responsible for Van Ness's tony atmosphere.

2

The Galaxy also pioneered an increase in the variety and visibility of the fare offered in theaters beyond popcorn, soda, and candy. The notion developed for the Galaxy was to present different upscale food options at attractive and decentralized concessions that added profit to the theater owner's bottom line and diversity to the moviegoing experience.

6

CITYWALK EAST
UNIVERSAL CITY, CALIFORNIA

In June 1995, KMD won a competition for a 60,000-square-foot (5,400-square-meter) expansion of Citywalk, the retail and entertainment complex at Universal Studios. An adjunct to the largest film and television studio in the world, Citywalk attracts more than nine million visitors each year. The program specified the extension of Citywalk eastward, beyond the existing Cinema Plaza, with its 24-screen cineplex and through a newly constructed parking garage.

A key objective in the Citywalk East project was integrating the new retail and entertainment facilities with a recently constructed Hard Rock Cafe and a planned Showmax theater both fronting on Cinema Plaza. Another major design consideration was the addition of scaling elements and a finer grain of detail to the existing plaza.

Taking these objectives into account, KMD's design set out to reinvent the Citywalk experience, to make it fresh—seamlessly integrate it with the existing style without being slavishly imitative of it. The scheme as developed evokes images of an "idealized" L.A. via environmental panoramas and reality-based urban experiences. The design is also less reliant on the megagraphics integral to Phase I, with facades suggesting vistas of the adjacent Hollywood hills that serve as a backdrop to the site.

To give increased visibility to tenants of the Citywalk addition, the new retail structure incorporates two dramatic towers which both terminate and complete the view corridor across Cinema Plaza, and beckon visitors to explore Citywalk's newest district. Another innovation, a curving street looping around existing structures on the east side of Cinema Plaza, serves both to avoid a cul-de-sac and to mitigate any possible obstruction by existing structures.

3

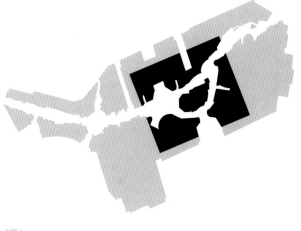

SITE I

SITE II

1   THE PHASE 2 PLAN INCORPORATES BOTH STREET AND
    PIAZZA TO EVOKE AN URBAN EXPERIENCE INTENSIFIED
    BY LIGHTING AND DRAMATIC ARCHITECTURE.

2   THE OVERALL EXPERIENCE IS ONE OF BRINGING
    TOGETHER THE IMAGES PEOPLE LIKE IN CITIES WITH THE
    ENTERTAINMENT AND RETAIL THEMES OF L.A. TODAY.

3   SUPER GRAPHICS, COLORFUL LIGHTING, AND BOLD
    SIGNAGE UNDERSCORE THE L.A. EXPERIENCE OF CITYWALK.

ONE COLORADO

OLD PASADENA, CALIFORNIA

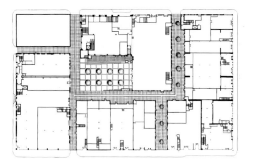

FIRST FLOOR

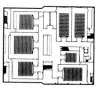

LOWER LEVEL

Envisioned as the cornerstone of Old Pasadena's urban revival, the One Colorado retail, entertainment, and office complex successfully preserves an historic commercial block, while creating an exciting retail environment that has drawn a new mix of people to a previously blighted neighborhood. The project undertook the renovation of seventeen historic buildings, including Pasadena's original city hall and jail, into a consolidated complex suited to contemporary use.

Moving beyond the conventional "covered mall" concept, KMD created a central plaza with circulation provided through existing back alleys that were transformed into paved outdoor walkways. The heart of One Colorado is a brick-paved outdoor plaza fronted by open-air dining areas and a second-level terrace which serves as a central meeting place and spot for people-watching.

One Colorado preserves a rich historic character, while incorporating into the block a new building housing an eight-screen underground theater with restaurants, shops, and offices built on two levels above. The original brick mercantile facades were restored to their original state, which required meticulous cleaning and repair of the brick. Simple details, such as colorful awnings, planters, and greenery and new historically accurate light fixtures add to the aesthetics. Restoration of the buildings required Pasadena Historical Society approval and earthquake retrofitting.

New storefronts on Colorado Boulevard were created by integrating the building's original design with an innovative interior floor structure based on an "up and down" design scheme. This arrangement allows visitors to walk into One Colorado at ground level, then walk up or down several steps to other shopping levels, creating two levels of ground floor retail.

One Colorado's appealing mix of uses has made it a popular destination, and the comfortable, inviting surroundings have the effect of making visitors want to linger. Whether enjoying a burger and shake, sipping a cappuccino at an outdoor cafe, or shopping in the many stores, local residents and visitors alike have taken to this revitalized environment.

1   RENOVATED STOREFRONTS ALONG
    COLORADO BOULEVARD

2   WHAT WAS ONCE A SERVICE ALLEY HAS
    BECOME AN INVITING ENTRANCE TO SHOPS.

4

5

6

3

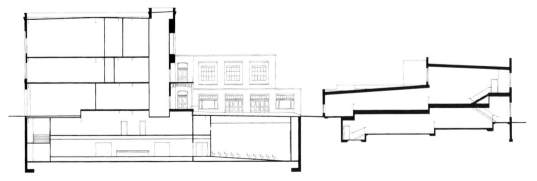

SECTION

MYCAL THEATERS

JAPAN

Throughout the late '80s and early '90s, the movie business in Japan was dying. The situation was similar to that in the U.S. and Europe a decade earlier when declining attendance, increased ticket prices, and competition from television equalled gloomy forecasts about the future of the movies. During that same time in the U.S. and Europe the fortunes of the movie business were reversed both by the spread of suburban shopping center multiplex theaters and by a revival of the movie blockbuster. In Japan however, with the majority of cinemas owned by movie studios and tending to show a limited range of film, attendance continued to fall. The response in the historically noncompetitive Japanese movie business was to raise ticket prices.

In early 1992 Warner Bros. formed a partnership with Nichii Co. Ltd. to develop a concept for Warner Mycal multiplex movie theaters in Japanese shopping centers, the same formula that had worked so well in the United States. KMD, fresh from its remarkable success with San Francisco's Galaxy Theater, was brought in as the design architect.

1 PLAYFUL NEON BRIGHTENS AND ACTIVATES THE FACADE.

2 THE LIGHTED GLASS ROTUNDA BOTTLES THE EXCITEMENT OF MOVIEGOING.

Between 1993 and 1995, seven KMD-designed multiplexes—each with six to eight screens and seating for 1,200–2,100 people—were built in suburban areas throughout Japan. It was the first time in Japan in years that the number of screens increased and the number of moviegoers climbed significantly.

The KMD concept was an elaboration on the Galaxy theme. The idea was to bring Hollywood to Japan and give movie houses the star quality that had made the American film industry a commercial draw worldwide. Utilizing neon, grand staircases, reflective surfaces, and celebratory lobbies, KMD's theater designs brought the excitement of the movies themselves out into the ticket, concession, and entry areas. Large ocular windows, glass window walls, and glowing signage brought the movie message outside to the street.

3   BRIGHT NEON AND HIGHLY REFLECTIVE SURFACES PUNCTUATE THE
    DRAMATIC LOBBY OF THIS CINEMA.

4   CONCESSIONS REFLECT THE EXCITEMENT OF GOING TO THE MOVIES.

5   THE FACADE ACTIVELY ANNOUNCES THE ENTERTAINMENT WITHIN.

5

SAMSUNG ELECTRONICS BUNDANG BUILDING

SUNGNAM, SOUTH KOREA

Designed for entertainment uses including a cinema, restaurants, and arcade, the six-story Bundang Building in Sungnam, a new town outside of Seoul, Korea, also defines the edge of a public plaza between a train station and one of the city's major streets. A bowed curtain wall is the main architectural feature along the plaza, behind which is a six-story escalator lobby connecting all internal levels of the building.

This glazed facade faces the pedestrian plaza and is designed to create a dramatic architectural statement during the day. At night, the facade becomes a transparent window into the activities within, the intent of which is to capture the attention of the customer and convey a clear sense of the entertainment values that await. In developing this design, KMD drew from the lights, color, and action of New York's Time Square. And like Times Square, the use of the buildings as billboard along with supersized signage evokes the tradition of advertising as entertainment.

Utilizing the latest audiovisual technology, the building becomes a performance stage playing to the facing plaza. Other devices including laser projection from pylons in the plaza, strobe lights located in the truss or embedded in the plaza surface, and giant-screen media displays complete the riveting entertainment statement of the design.

1   THE BUILDING AS ENTERTAINMENT; THE SAMSUNG
PROJECT EMPHASIZES LIGHTS AND ACTION.

1 IN THE TRADITION OF SOUTH AMERICAN 20TH
   CENTURY ARCHITECTURE, PANAMBI'S STYLE IS
   MODERNIST, SOFTENED BY HUMANIZING DETAILS
   AND RICH LANDSCAPING.

2 THE SINUOUS CURVE THAT FORMS THE MAJOR
   THOROUGH FARE OF PANAMBI HAS ITS BASE IN KMD
   STUDIES THAT INDICATE THAT PEOPLE ENJOY CURVING
   PASSAGES MORE THAN LONG STRAIGHT STREETS.

São Paulo is Brazil's largest city, an industrial and cultural mecca that boasts four universities, the largest industrial base in South America, and 12 million people who display diverse interests and enthusiastic support of the city's many cultural institutions.

With these factors in mind, KMD's charge was to create an "urban village" along Avenida Das Nacoes Unidas in the São Paulo suburbs, one that would unite the lush natural Brazilian greenery with the modern realities of office and residential towers, retail stores, and entertainment centers. In addition all of the project's elements needed to convey an air of sophistication and "sense of place" that would appeal to São Paulo's diverse and cosmpolitan inhabitants.

The resulting Panambi Development, planned to start construction in 1998, combines the best of all worlds. The 2-million-square-foot (180,000-square-meter) project consists of four 7–18 story office towers, a 216,000-square-foot (20,000-square-meter), 300-room hotel, four 8–14 story residential towers, a complex of executive apartments, and a retail center and multiscreen cinema. The many elements are divided into commercial and residential zones linked by a cultural center and landscaped gardens.

In keeping with KMD's philosophy of creating celebratory space and a sense of arrival via the architecture of a public space, Panambi is situated between two substantial open plazas. One plaza is anchored by an 89,000-square-foot (8,000-square-meter) cultural center. The second sits in the center of the cinema, hotel, and office towers. A scripted pedestrian street, lined with retail shops, links the two plazas.

The sprawling retail strip sits atop a raised podium that provides shoppers a view of both plazas. Grand ornamental staircases and cascading tropical gardens are the backdrop for this area of Panambi Development.

The residential towers, which encompass the architecture of the neighboring structures, are finished with detailing and trim derived from native materials. Residents enjoy views of a nearby public park and its small central lake. At the heart of the residential area are a social club and a health club.

KMD's Panambi Development successfully blends high-density urban design with the natural landscape of suburban São Paulo.

3 THE PLANNING CONCEPTS OF PANAMBI JUXTAPOSE
   LARGE BUILDING BLOCKS WITH HUMANIZING
   INFLUENCES OF SMALLER BUILDINGS, LANDSCAPING,
   AND OPEN SPACE.

4 THE OVERALL PLAN AND PLACEMENT OF BUILDINGS
   HELPS CREATE A SENSE OF PLACE WITHOUT LIMITING
   A DESIRED FEELING OF OPENNESS.

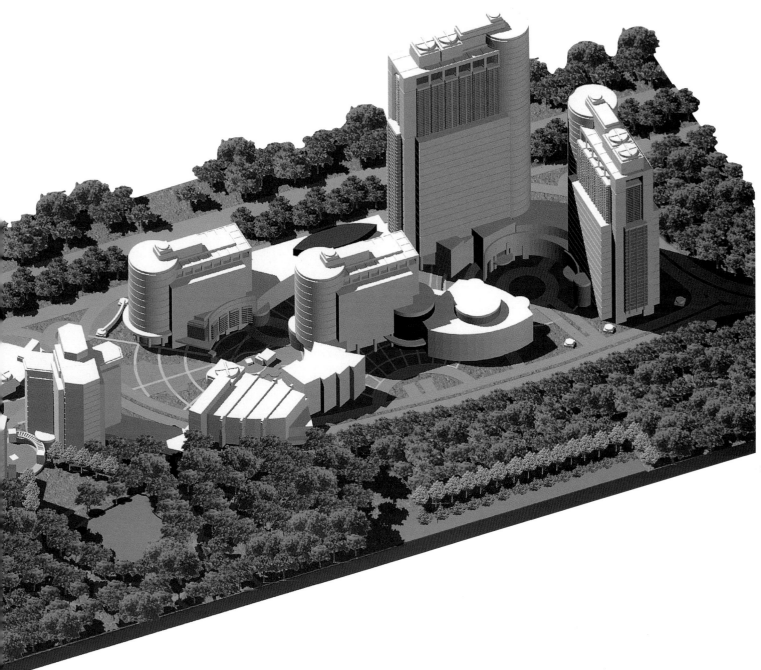

2

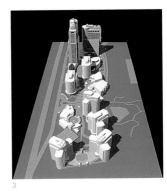

3

4

1   A TOTAL VISION OF TAICHUNG

2   THE FASCINATION OF A NEW RETAIL EXPERIENCE

3   APPROACHING THE TAICHUNG URBAN AGORA

4   SINUOUS CURVES OFFER NEW PATHS OF DISCOVERY, WHILE OPENING
    ADDITIONAL RETAIL SPACE.

Planned for a 26-acre (9-hectare) site on a former sugar refinery in this small west-central city in Taipei, the Taichung Central Business District concept calls for the development of a vital urban village deriving from design principles and characteristics of many of the world's most successful public retail streets. Including elements such as a sugar museum, aquarium, sports-themed retail village, fashion court and food villages, the plan calls for the creation of a destination appeal for the region and beyond while reinforcing the vitality of the existing Taichung business district.

Recognizing that it will take many years for the total vision of the Taichung CBD to be realized, incremental phasing has been carefully evaluated from both the point of view of critical mass and economic infrastructure investment. In the initial phase, unique retail and entertainment districts will be developed along a serpentine pedestrian path named Discovery Street. This will link a new Gateway Plaza and the nearby Taichung CBD to future phases on the south and east. Incremental mixed-use development is planned for the eastern edge of this site. Consisting of office, hotel, and retail uses, this phase will create a strong urban street edge along the major north/south artery. Further extension of Discovery Street will help create a unified development district.

The retail concept keys off of Discovery Street as the armature which links the northern and southern gateways of the site. Rather than following a straight line, a wavelike path winds through the length of the project. The practical benefit of this design element is that it increases the amount of retail frontage along the street while effectively controlling the lease depths.

This approach also creates an exhilarating experience of exploration and ever-changing vistas as one walks the length of Discovery Street. And because the entire project cannot be seen from any one location, the ability to create distinct "themed" districts becomes possible. Shops and restaurants line the street between each plaza, providing a continuous series of varied experiences in shopping and entertainment. And recalling the former use of the site, a tower element reminiscent of sugar refinery equipment occupies a prominent position within the Gateway Plaza, which will act as a major ceremonial civic gathering place for Taichung and connect the project to surrounding urban areas.

JAMES C. FLOOD BUILDING

SAN FRANCISCO, CALIFORNIA

A monument to late-nineteenth century civic pride and commercial success, San Francisco's Flood Building had the distinction of being the largest and tallest building west of the Mississippi at the time of its completion in 1904. Since then, this dignified downtown landmark has lived through many an incarnation—most recently, a KMD-designed renovation that has restored this downtown landmark to its original elegance.

The lower three floors of this grand structure were reorganized to create new and very valuable retail square footage: the most dramatic part of a large-scale renovation, which also restored and reframed the entire exterior.

Designed by architect Albert Pissis and built in honor of Nevada silver baron James C. Flood, the twelve-story tower at the corner of Powell and Market streets was originally a hotel. While the earthquake of 1906 did not cause significant damage to the flatiron-style structure, subsequent fires damaged the building's interior. In addition to post-quake reconstruction, the Flood building was significantly altered in 1919, 1936, and again in 1952.

While the 1952 renovation created the world's largest Woolworth's variety store in the basement, ground, and second floors, it also replaced the building's original arched storefront with a modernist faux-granite base. Also contributing to the deterioration of the building's original qualities was the severe weather damage of the Flood's Colusa sandstone facade. Attempts in the 1930s to protect the stone with waterproof paint exacerbated the damage by preventing evaporation.

At the behest of building owner and family heir, Jim Flood, KMD began renovation of the landmark in 1992. The restoration had two goals: to return the storefront and retail section of the building to its pre-1952, multitenant condition and to restore the sandstone facade on the building's upper levels to its original beauty.

1

2

JAMES C. FLOOD BUILDING

Surfaces on the basement, ground, and second floors were stripped to floor slabs and columns, and electrical and plumbing systems were replaced. A central corridor was constructed to act as a spine for the retail area, facilitating future alteration. A loading dock and easily accessible rest rooms were also added.

The four storefront arches that had been destroyed were replaced by castings taken from a remaining arch. Metal and glass curtain walls were installed between the arches to create a modern storefront, although its mullion patterns, transom-level windows, and awnings are reminiscent of the original storefront. A flat canopy at the building's prominent corner copies a similar canopy from the 1920s.

Where possible, the damaged sandstone was repaired and retooled or patched with Portland cement to approximate its original condition. Balusters that were damaged beyond repair were replaced with polymer concrete cast from molds of undamaged originals. Similarly, parapets that were beyond repair were carved back three to five inches to a sound surface, then covered with polymer concrete casts. Flat wall areas were faced with lath and stucco.

The Flood building is again a favorite of tourists at the adjacent cable car turnaround on Powell Street, its retail and restoration goals successfully met.

5

6

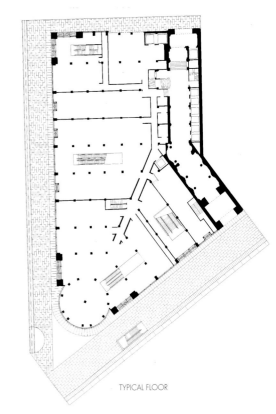

TYPICAL FLOOR

PASSY PLAZA

In 1991 KMD was commissioned to transform the lower floors of a former department store on the Rue Passy in Paris's 16th Arrondisement into a 120,000-square-foot (1,100-square-meter), multitenant, high-end retail arcade. Passy Plaza serves as a retail anchor for a mixed-use development that includes 260 luxury condominiums, a terraced garden, and parking garage. The project was done in collaboration with Bechu Architects, Ltd., Paris.

Transferring the concept of celebratory retail across the Atlantic, KMD designers drew on Paris's indigenous early-1900s, Belle Époque period for detail and theme to create a space reminiscent of outdoor Parisian market streets. Centered around two glass rotundas, the natural light from which would enhance the impression of chic street-level shopping, the arcade's high-end retail shops were designed with distinctive individual storefronts. This helped establish separate identities for the stores as well as a dramatic sense of place for the arcade.

A celebratory double helix staircase is the centerpiece of the main rotunda, while loggias, balconies, and terraces establish a visual complexity and a sense of discovery that maintains a sense of freshness and encourages return visits. Similarly, a specialty food market on the lower level was designed to enhance the sense that Passy Plaza was a destination rather than simply a place to buy things.

Passy Plaza's interior sense of celebration was brought outside through the use of elegant storefront space along the building's streetfront. This—and a flying glass canopy at the entrance—was designed to literally draw the eye to the arcade's entryway and to draw shoppers inside what, in 1994, became one of Paris's most exciting new retail experiences.

1   THROUGH THE INSERTION OF RETAIL AT THE STREET AND SUBSURFACE LEVELS, THIS OLDER APARTMENT BLOCK IS ENLIVENED.

2   THE ENTRANCE CANOPY, STRATEGICALLY PLACED AT A BUSY CORNER, EVOKES THE ART NOUVEAU TRADITION OF PARIS MÉTRO STATIONS.

2

3   THE RETAIL DEVELOPMENT TAKES ADVANTAGE OF THE
    OLDER BUILDING'S RICH DETAILS AND INDIVIDUALITY.

4   THE CENTRAL STAIRCASE FORMS THE CORE OF
    PASSY PLAZA'S SHOPPING EXPERIENCE.

5   AT THE CENTER OF THE SHOPPING COMPLEX IS A
    SINUOUS DOUBLE STAIRCASE INVITING A COMFORTABLE
    FLOW BETWEEN THE MALL'S TWO LEVELS.

6   THE CENTRAL STAIRCASES FORM A LIVELY MEETING PLACE
    AND SERVE AS THE AXIS OF ACTIVITY IN THIS NEWLY
    REVITALIZED URBAN CENTER.

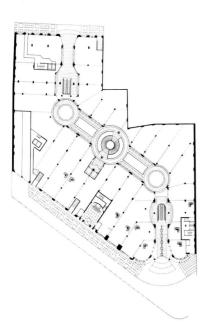

SITE

3

4

5

SELECTED CHRONOLOGY

1968 MARIN GENERAL HOSPITAL
GREENBRAE, CALIFORNIA
PP. 102-105

MARTIN LUTHER KING SQUARE
SAN FRANCISCO. CALIFORNIA

1973 ST. MARK'S HOSPITAL
SALT LAKE CITY. UTAH

1975 THE MARTINELLI HOUSE
SAN RAFAEL, CALIFORNIA

1976 HUDSON-ON-MEMORIAL
HOUSTON, TEXAS

ST. VINCENT HOSPITAL
SANTA FE. NEW MEXICO

1977 TOMALES BAY
TOMALES BAY, CALIFORNIA

**1978 ANOKA METROPOLITAN
REGIONAL TREATMENT CENTER**
ANOKA, MINNESOTA

**ART CENTRE HOSPITAL
MENTAL HEALTH UNIT**
DETROIT, MICHIGAN

**CONTRA COSTA COUNTY
ADULT DETENTION FACILITY**
MARTINEZ, CALIFORNIA

EMANUEL HOSPITAL
PORTLAND, OREGON

OMAHA BUILDING
OMAHA, NEBRASKA

1979 FRENCHMAN'S CREEK
HOUSTON, TEXAS

HALLIDIE BUILDING
SAN FRANCISCO. CALIFORNIA

WALNUT CREEK CENTER I
WALNUT CREEK, CALIFORNIA

1980 LA GALLERIA
SAN FRANCISCO, CALIFORNIA

SAN RAFAEL COMMONS
SAN RAFAEL, CALIFORNIA

1981 CHILDREN'S HOSPITAL
DENVER, COLORADO

MERCY HEALTH CAMPUS
BAKERSFIELD, CALIFORNIA
PP. 106-109

1982 CLEVELAND ARCADE
CLEVELAND, OHIO

GALLERIA PARK HOTEL
SAN FRANCISCO, CALIFORNIA

GIFT CENTER
SAN FRANCISCO, CALIFORNIA

**KOLB RESEARCH CENTER,
COLUMBIA UNIVERSITY**
NEW YORK, NEW YORK

SAN JOSE MEDICAL CENTER
SAN JOSE, CALIFORNIA

WALNUT CREEK CENTER II
WALNUT CREEK, CALIFORNIA

1983 MAGNOLIA BUILDING
DALLAS, TEXAS

VISTA HILL HOSPITAL
CHULA VISTA, CALIFORNIA

1984 ALPINE SQUARE
WALNUT CREEK, CALIFORNIA

**BRIGHAM & WOMEN'S
HOSPITAL**
BOSTON, MASSACHUSETTS
PP. 132-137

CAMINO ALTO COURT
MILL VALLEY, CALIFORNIA

GALAXY THEATER
SAN FRANCISCO, CALIFORNIA
PP. 172-175

ST. JOSEPH'S HOSPITAL
MENTAL HEALTH CENTER
LANCASTER, PENNSYLVANIA

WASHINGTON/MONTGOMERY
TOWER
SAN FRANCISCO, CALIFORNIA
PP. 70-73

1985 INTERNATIONAL
MARKET SQUARE
MINNEAPOLIS, MINNESOTA
PP. 52-55

THE KOLL CENTER BAYSHORE
SAN JOSE, CALIFORNIA

LAWRENCE LIVERMORE
LABORATORIES
LIVERMORE, CALIFORNIA

SETON MEDICAL CENTER
DALY CITY, CALIFORNIA

ST. MARY'S HOSPITAL
SAN FRANCISCO, CALIFORNIA

TISHMAN OFFICE CENTER
WALNUT CREEK, CALIFORNIA

UNION TERMINAL
DENVER, COLORADO

1986 CALIFORNIA PLAZA
WALNUT CREEK, CALIFORNIA

DEARBORN STATION
CHICAGO, LLLINOIS

ICE HOUSE I
DENVER, COLORADO

MARINA VALLARTA
PUERTO VALLARTA, MEXICO

PACIFIC PRESBYTERIAN
PROFESSIONAL BUILDING
SAN FRANCISCO, CALIFORNIA

PARK HILL
SAN FRANCISCO, CALIFORNIA

PROVIDENCE MEDICAL CENTER
OLYMPIA, WASHINGTON

ST. FRANCIS PLACE
SAN FRANCISCO, CALIFORNIA

ST. JOSEPH'S HOSPITAL
BELLINGHAM, WASHINGTON

STEVENSON PLACE
SAN FRANCISCO, CALIFORNIA

1987 1333 NORTH CALIFORNIA
BOULEVARD
WALNUT CREEK, CALIFORNIA

CALIFORNIA MEDICAL CENTER
LOS ANGELES, CALIFORNIA
PP. 142-145

CENTRAL PLAZA
SAN FRANCISCO, CALIFORNIA
PP. 74-75

1988 CONTRACT CENTER
SAN FRANCISCO, CALIFORNIA

ONE BUSH STREET
SAN FRANCISCO, CALIFORNIA

SANTA CLARA VALLEY
MEDICAL CENTER
SAN JOSE, CALIFORNIA

SUTTER CENTER
FOR PSYCHIATRY
SACRAMENTO, CALIFORNIA

UCI, CROSS CULTURAL CENTER
UNIVERSITY OF CALIFORNIA,IRVINE

1989 49 STEVENSON
SAN FRANCISCO, CALIFORNIA

CENTRAL STOCKTON PLAN
STOCKTON, CALIFORNIA 1989

CHECKERS HOTEL
LOS ANGELES, CALIFORNIA

COTTONWOOD HOSPITAL
CENTER FOR WOMEN'S HEALTH
MURRAY. UTAH

FEDERAL RESERVE
BANK BUILDING
SAN FRANCISCO, CALIFORNIA

SCHOOL OF INTERNATIONAL
RELATIONS AND PACIFIC STUDIES
UNIVERSITY OF CALIFORNIA, SAN DIEGO
PP. 42-47

PELICAN BAY STATE PRISON
CRESCENT CITY, CALIFORNIA

PRICE CENTER
UNIVERSITY OF CALIFORNIA, SAN DIEGO
PP. 164-171

SAN DIEGO COUNTY
HEALTH SERVICES
SAN DIEGO, CALIFORNIA

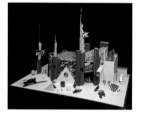

SANTA FE BUSINESS PARK
SANTA FE, NEW MEXICO

SUTTER MATERNITY AND
SURGERY CENTER
SANTA CRUZ, CALIFORNIA
PP. 152-155

UCI OTSU
OTSU, JAPAN

UCSF MEDICAL OFFICE
BUILDING
SAN FRANCISCO, CALIFORNIA

U.S. WWII MEMORIAL
SAIPAN, COMMONWEALTH OF
NORTHERN MARIANA ISLANDS

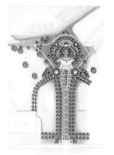

1997 AMC SARATOGA
SAN JOSE, CALIFORNIA

BANCO BITAL DATA CENTER
TOLUCA, STATE OF MEXICO

TOM BRADLEY
INTERNATIONAL TERMINAL
LOS ANGELES INTERNATIONAL AIRPORT

CHANG BING MEDICAL CENTER
LUKANG, TAIWAN

CHEIL GENERAL HOSPITAL
SEOUL, SOUTH KOREA
PP. 110-113

DALHEL KYOTO DESIGN CENTER
KYOTO, JAPAN

DEL PARQUE
SANTA FE, MEXICO

DUKE UNIVERSITY
CHILDREN'S HEALTH CENTER
DURHAM, NORTH CAROLINA

FDA LABORATORY AND
OFFICE FACILITY
QUEENS, NEW YORK

GOODRICH/RIQUELME
Y ASOCIADOS LAW FIRM
MEXICO CITY, MEXICO

LANE COUNTY JUVENILE
JUSTICE CENTER
EUGENE, OREGON

LITTLE COMPANY OF MARY
HOSPITAL
TORRANCE, CALIFORNIA

MERDEKA SQUARE
KUALA LUMPUR, MALAYSIA

MIHAMA CINEMA COMPLEX
OKINAWA, JAPAN

PRESIDIO GOLF & CLUBHOUSE
SAN FRANCISCO, CALIFORNIA

PROVIDENCE MEDICAL CENTER
MILWAUKIE, OREGON

RESIDENTIAL SANTA FE
SANTA FE, MEXICO

RILEY OUTPATIENT CENTER
INDIANA UNIVERSITY
MEDICAL CENTER
INDIANAPOLIS, INDIANA

SAMSUNG ELECTRONICS
BUNDANG BUILDING
SEOUL, KOREA
PP. 186-187

SAN FERNANDO COURTHOUSE
SAN FERNANDO, CALIFORNIA

SAN FRANCISCO STATE
UNIVERSITY STUDENT CENTER
SAN FRANCISCO, CALIFORNIA

SAN MATEO COUNTY
MUNICIPAL COURTS
REDWOOD CITY, CALIFORNIA

SUTTER GENERAL HOSPITAL
SACRAMENTO, CALIFORNIA

TAICHUNG REGIONAL CENTER
TAIPEI, TAIWAN
PP. 190-191

TRON LAB
UNIVERSITY OF CALIFORNIA
LOS ANGELES, CALIFORNIA

UNIVERSITY OF ALASKA
FAIRBANKS
FAIRBANKS, ALASKA

1998 BALMORAL CRESCENT
SINGAPORE

EWE BOON ROAD
SINGAPORE

KLAMATH COUNTY
COURTHOUSE
KLAMATH FALLS, OREGON

PANAMBI MASTER PLAN
SÃO PAULO, BRAZIL
PP. 188-189

TAEJON RAIL STATION
TAEJON, KOREA

UNIVERSITY OF CALIFORNIA
OFFICE OF THE PRESIDENT
OAKLAND, CALIFORNIA

1999 SHANGHAI INTERNATIONAL
BUSINESS CENTER/PLAZA
SHANGHAI, CHINA
PP. 80-81

2000 KOOKMIN BANK
HEADQUARTERS BUILDING
SEOUL, SOUTH KOREA
PP. 66-69

KMD has built its practice on the creativity and innovative talents of key design, technical, and management professionals. The core staff of these professionals is represented by the titled leaders of the firm, Directors, Senior Associates, and Associates. As of this printing, this core group is represented by the following individuals.

DIRECTORS	SENIOR ASSOCIATES	ASSOCIATES
Vernon L. Almon	Phillip H. Bahr	Arnel C. Agodon
Kenneth A. Caldwell	John Baker	Peter D. Alef
Jeffrey B. Causey	Thomas E. Beggs	Michael L. Beaman
William J. D'Elia	Elizabeth M. Chaney	Carolyn J. Bouget
Mohinder S. Datta	Nancy Classen	David Bryant
James R. Diaz	Robert R. Fierro	Gregory Y. Chang
Thomas A. Gross	Katy Taylor Ford	Monica Clarke
David Hobstetter	Kelly Galloway	Janet Corah
Steven A. Kelley	Francis Gough	Dianne M. Davis
Roy S. Latka	Michael Green	Victor R. DeSantis
Fred Lee	Philip C. Griffen	Lari Maria Diaz
Rob Matthew	Mark Henderson	Tim Firman
Herb McLaughlin	Sandra L. Hing	Sandy Grimm
Howard F. McNenny	Wray Humphrey	Greg K. Iboshi
Mark R. Miller	Morten Jensen	MacDonald H. Jackson
Ken Minohara	John Jex	Takeshi Kikuchi
James W. Mueller	Eugene S. Jung	David H. Lang
John Newcomb	John F. Marx	Jennifer J. Lin
Juan Diego Perez-Vargas	Sang Kee Min	Dorothy A. Lloyd
James B. Richardson	Ken Mineau	John A. MacAllister
Mel Schenck	Mark F. O'Dell	John C. Paape
Mackenzie Skene	Elaine C. Pavia	Tom Patterson
Michael E. Stinetorf	Steven Ryder	Donna Pinto
Thomas A. Wornson	Frederick W. Schreck	Beth S. Radovanovich
Gary Zuke	John Scott	Janell Robinett
	Richard D. H. Sheng	Mark J. Ryan
	Leonardo D. Srichantra	Neal J. Z. Schwartz
	Anastasio Stathopoulos	Mark J. Seiberlich
	Dean John Vlahos	Jan Vargo
	Chet Wing	Stephen K. Wong
	Lena Ning Zhang	

The Historic Architecture of Late Nineteenth Century Philadelphia, 1964.

Community Health Center, Vol 1: Planning, Programming and Design for the Community Mental Health Center. United States National Institute of Mental Health, 1966.

Community Health Center, Vol 2: Planning, Programming and Design for the Community Mental Health Center. United States National Institute of Mental Health, 1966.

Laboratory Use Patterns and Design Standards, 1967.

Efficiency of Design of Hospital Nursing Units, 1968.

Hospital Prototypes, 1968.

Social Patterns and Design for Street Life, 1968.

Evaluation of Alternate Architectural Plans Using Numerical Grading Systems, 1969.

Operating Experience in Single Care Bedroom, 1969.

Post Occupancy Study of Marin Community Medical Center, 1969.

Systems Analysis for Comparing Alternative Design Solutions, 1969.

Function and Imagery of Architecture and Furnishings in Hospital Public Spaces, 1970.

Patterns of Obsolescence in Hospitals, 1970

Small Schools, Efficiency and Practicality, 1970.

Materials Handling Systems Evaluation, 1971.

Transport Systems for Hospitals, 1972.

Principles of Design and Impacts on Operating Costs of Medical Office Buildings, 1973.

Napa/ Sonoma State Hospitals—A Master Utilization Plan of Various Futures for Two California State Hospitals, 1976.

Manhattanization Study, 1978.

Facility Programming: Methods and Applications. Preiser, Wolfgang, Ed., 1978.

Facilities Trends in Hospital Diversification, 1978.

Hilo Hospital, an Analysis of Nursing Unit Size, Staffing, Linkage and Shape, 1978.

Comparative Jail Study, A Study of Six Detention Facilities: Lane County, Contra Costa County, Kane County, Bernalillo, Durango and Boulder, 1979.

Obsolescence and Hospital Design, 1979.

Post Occupancy Study Leads to Insights on Elderly Housing with Judith Bernstein and Laurie Hart. Martinelli House, 1979.

Conversion of Acute Hospitals to Long-Term Care Institutions— The Problems and Possibilities, 1980.

Humanistic Architecture for Mental Health. A Special Symposium. American Psychiatric Association, 1980.

Rehab/New Construction: Development and Evaluation Techniques, 1980.

Tivoli (Denmark) Amusement Parks Study for Palisades, New Jersey, 1980.

Designing Facilities Around Market Demand. Association of Mental Health Administrators, San Diego, 1981.

Living Over the Office: The Mixed-Use High-Rise Comes of Age by Benjamin Claven, 1982.

Obsolescence and Hospital Design, 1982.

Diversification Opportunities—Land, Facilities and Energy Systems as a Means to Hospital Diversification, 1982.

Planning for Intensive Care Centers, 1982.

Facilities Trends in Hospital Diversification. (AHA Conference, San Francisco), 1983.

Architecture for Health: Determining Hospital Space Requirements. Conference, Los Angeles, Feb. 4, 1984.

Tall Buildings, Tight Streets, 1985.

Urban Agoras, 1985.

Denver Central Area Plan, 1985.

Camino Alto Court—Post Occupancy Evaluation, 1985.

The Courts at Clinton, a Study of Socialization at a New York State Prison, 1985.

Alternative Birthing Center. Design and Programming Reader, 1986.

Nowhere to Run—American Jail Association, 1989.

Contra Costa County Main Detention Facility—Post Occupancy Evaluation, 1989.

Central Valley Conference, California, 1990.

Women's Facilities Study, Volume 1, 1990.

Giving Something Back; Innovation; Slopopolis; Agoras; Future of Retail; Renovation; National Trust for Historic Preservation Annual Conference, 1991.

Hidden LA: An Investigation into Los Angeles great Overlooked Architecture (paper & bus tour), 1991.

A Vision for Downtown Oakland, 1991.

Development outside the United States—Insights and Observations (Urban Land Institute), 1992.

Re-use Applications for De-commissioned Airbases, Mather Air Force Base, Sacramento, California, 1992.

Sacramento Urban Design Plan: Downtown Plan, Sacramento Hilltop Plan, Signal Hill California, 1992.

Westlake/MacArthur Red Line Station Master Plan, Los Angeles, California, 1993.

Howard Street Development Study, 1993.

Fisherman's Wharf Housing: Retail Implications, 1994.

North Beach Place Plan Process and Design Guidelines, San Francisco, California, 1994.

Las Vegas Federal Building and Courthouse—Research Proposal to the GSA, 1994.

MacArthur BART Station Planning Process, Oakland, California, 1995.

Modern Courthouse—Designing for the 21st Century, 1996.

Modern Courthouse—How Technology will impact the future of Courthouse Design, 1996.

Santa Clara Asset Management Plan, 1996.

Publication about KMD's research, theory and work has equaled or exceeded that of any architecture firm in this country. Following is a selected listing of magazine articles published about and by the firm.

PRACTICE AND DESIGN

"Collaborations on the Rise—and the Need for Careful Agreements." *Architectural Record.*

"Controlling Delay Claims." *Architectural Record.*

"LA: The City." *Architectural Review.*

"Reinventing Slopopolis." *Architecture.*

"Wooing the Government Tenant." *Building Operating Management.*

"Putting the Public in Public Places." *Buildings.*

"Tall Buildings, Tight Streets." *Northwest Land Use Review.*

"New Town-Gown Planning." *Planning for Higher Education.*

"Celebrating Urban Gathering Places." *Urban Land.*

GENERAL PROJECTS

"An Up-to-Date Movie Place." *Architectural Record.*

"Good-Guy Modern." *Architectural Record.*

"Planning for the Urban Marketplace." *Architectural Record.*

"Postoccupancy Study. Leads to Insights on Elderly Housing." *Architectural Record.*

"Reshaping the San Francisco Skyline." *Architectural Record.*

"Award Winning and Other Outstanding School and University Buildings." *AS&U Architectural Portfolio*

"The Architecture of Community." *Association of College Unions.*

"NAHB Awards of Excellence." Building Design & Construction.

"Reigning Supreme." *Contract Design.*

"Two Rodeo Drive The Feeling of Europe in Beverly Hills." *Designers West.*

"Rainbow Crew Builds GSA Complex." *Engineering News Record.*

"Project File: Plaza Park Hotel." *Facilities Planning News.*

"Cities Revitalize." *Interiors.*

"Historicist 'Via Rodeo' for Beverly Hills." *Progressive Architecture.*

"UC Builds, San Diego." *Progressive Architecture.*

"San Diego's Graduate School." *School and College.*

"New, Improved Rodeo Drive." *Travel & Leisure.*

"Nice Trick—Two Ground Floors at Two Rodeo Drive." *Urban Land.*

"Reinventing Federal Procurement Practices—The Oakland Federal Building." *Urban Land.*

INTERNATIONAL

"East Meets West: When Architects Collaborate." *Architectural Record.*

"American Architects in Asia." *Architecture.*

"Come Home to Nagoya." *Contract Design.*

"Yukio Goes to Hollywood." *Contract Design.*

"Royal Washington Hotel." *Nikkei Architecture.*

"Urban Living for Senior Citizens" *Nikkei Architecture.*

"Japan—New Consumers, New Building Types." *Pacific Rim Business Digest.*

"Morning Park Chikaramachi." *Shin-Kenchiku.*

"Mays One Building—Two Tenant Building, Eddie Bauer and Tower Records, with Chicago-Style Facade." *Shoten Kenchiku.*

RENOVATION

"A 'Preservation Addict' Looks at the Practical Side of Rehabilitating for Profit." *Architectural Record.*

"International Market Square." *Baumeister.*

"Firm Pushes Renovation to Hilt; Converts Industrial Building to Top Commercial Use." *California Builder.*

"The Gift Center Lights Up San Francisco." *Commercial Renovation.*

"Pasadena Complex Wins Beautification Award." *Los Angeles Times.*

"Bank Fortress to Provide Access to San Francisco's Financial District." *Urban Land.*

HEALTHCARE AND MENTAL HEALTH

"Acute Care Stacked on Public Uses: An addition to serve severely ill patient also triggered an upgrade of amenities for the hospital as a whole." *Architectural Record.*

"Evolution and Evaluation of Environment for Mental Health." *Architectural Record.*

"The Hospital-Affiliated Medical Office Building." *Architectural Record.*

"Keeping Fit: Ambulatory Services, Building, Brigham and Women's Hospital." *Architectural Record.*

"Managing Acute Care." *Architectural Record.*

"The Monumental Headache. Overtly Monumental and Systematic Hospitals are Usually Functional Disasters." *Architectural Record.*

"Toward a More Humane Healthcare." *Architectural Record.*

"Designing for the Healthcare Process and Marketplace." *Architecture.*

"Medical Turnaround." *Architecture.*

"Oasis Healing." *Architecture.*

"How the American Hospital Changes Its Image." Mitchell Green. *Architecture & Urbanism.*

"Northwest's Largest Trauma Center." *Building Design & Construction.*

"New Hospital Designs Stress Looking Good." *Engineering News Record.*

"Psychiatric Facility—One with Nature." *Health Facilities Management.*

"Interior Design Supports Psychiatric Therapy." Hospitals.

"Designer-Construction Manager Team Needs Hard Coaching From Hospitals." *Modern Healthcare.*

IMAGE CREDITS

Russell Abraham Photography
CHRONOLOGY P. 203 RIGHT, TOP

Alexander Auerbach
TWO RODEO DRIVE 2,8,11

Richard Barnes
OAKLAND FEDERAL BUILDING 11
MARIN GENERAL HOSPITAL 1,4,6
ONE COLORADO 1,4-6
JAMES C. FLOOD BUILDING
CHRONOLOGY P. 203 LEFT

Michel Benichou
PASSY PLAZA 5

Gabriel Benzur, Inc.
GRADY MEMORIAL HOSPITAL 6,8,12,13,15

Paul Bielenberg
TWO RODEO DRIVE 1,3,7,10

Andy Boone
MYCAL THEATERS 1-2

Brady Architectural Photography
SCHOOL OF INTERNATIONAL RELATIONS
AND PACIFIC STUDIES 1-5,7-11
THE WILSHIRE 1,3,4,6
PRICE CENTER 4,5,6,11,13,14
UCSD MEDICAL CENTER 3

Calthorpe/Solomon
BUMI JAYA 4

Robert Canfield
SHANGHAI INTERNATIONAL
BUSINESS CENTER 2,4

W. Chin
CHRONOLOGY P. 200 CENTER, BOTTOM

Stanley Doctor
PURI JAYA 3
BUMI JAYA 3

Don Farrell Const. Photography
BRIGHAM AND WOMEN'S HOSPITAL 3

Soncin Gerometta
OAKLAND FEDERAL BUILDING 1

Jeff Goldberg/Esto
P. 9 TOP RIGHT
BUSINESS ADMINISTRATION
AND EDUCATION BUILDING,
PLAZA PARK,
MERCY SOUTHWEST HOSPITAL,
DECKER CENTER FOR
ADVANCED MEDICAL TREATMENT,
CHRONOLOGY P. 202 CENTER, BOTTOM

Franz Hall Architectural Photography
INTERNATIONAL MARKET SQUARE 1,7

Isao Harukami
P. 12 TOP LEFT
NADYA PARK
INTERNATIONAL DESIGN CENTER
1,3-12,14

David Hewitt/Anne Garrison
UCSD MEDICAL CENTER 1,2,5,6
PRICE CENTER 2
CHRONOLOGY P. 202 LEFT, BOTTOM

Fred Housel
HARBORVIEW MEDICAL CENTER

Douglas E. Jamieson
SHANGHAI INTERNATIONAL PLAZA 2,3
CHEIL GENERAL HOSPITAL 3

Michael Joyce
P. 17 TOP RIGHT

Donna Kempner
MARIN GENERAL HOSPITAL 3
PRICE CENTER 1,8,12,15,16
SCHOOL OF INTERNATIONAL RELATIONS
AND PACIFIC STUDIES 6

Sato Kogyo
ROYAL WASHINGTON HOTEL 2,7

Balthazar Korab
INTERNATIONAL MARKET SQUARE 4,6,8,9

Erich Ansel Koyama
SUTTER MATERNITY AND
SURGERY CENTER 1-4,6,7

Yasu Kurumada
NADYA PARK 1-7,9-15
INTERNATIONAL DESIGN CENTER
2,13,15

Mitsuo Matsuoka
NADYA PARK 8

Nick Merrick, Hedrich Blessing
PRICE CENTER 3,7,17,18
TITLE PAGE

Kokyu Miwa Photo Laboratory
K.K. NAKAZATO
CORPORATE HEADQUARTERS

S. S. Nagoya
MORNING PARK

Kazuo Natori
ROYAL WASHINGTON HOTEL 3-6,8

Michael O'Callahan
OAKLAND FEDERAL BUILDING 2,5-9,12

Sally Painter
MARIN GENERAL HOSPITAL 7
CALIFORNIA MEDICAL CENTER 1,3,9
PRICE CENTER 10

Sally Painter *(con't)*
CHRONOLOGY P. 200 CENTER TOP; RIGHT,
TOP; RIGHT,BOTTOM; P.201 CENTER,
MIDDLE; CENTER,BOTTOM; RIGHT,TOP;
RIGHT,BOTTOM; P. 202 LEFT, LOWER MIDDLE

Erhard Pfeiffer
ONE COLORADO 3

Paul Raftery
PASSY PLAZA 1,2,6

Tom Rider
CENTRAL PLAZA 2
MARIN GENERAL HOSPITAL 2,5

Rion C. Rizzo/Creative Sources
Photography/Atlanta
GRADY MEMORIAL HOSPITAL
1-5,7,9-11,14

Steve Rosenthal
BRIGHAM AND WOMEN'S HOSPITAL 2,4-13

Cesar Rubio
OAKLAND FEDERAL BUILDING 10

Neal Schwartz
SUTTER MATERNITY AND
SURGERY CENTER 5,8

Michael Sechman
KOOKMIN BANK
HEADQUARTERS BUILDING

Jim Simmons/Annette Del Zoppo
Photography
ONE COLORADO 2

Ron Starr
OAKLAND FEDERAL BUILDING 3

Tim Street-Porter
THE WILSHIRE 2,5

John Sutton
CALIFORNIA MEDICAL CENTER 4,5,7,8
GALAXY THEATER
INTERNATIONAL MARKET SQUARE 2
CHRONOLOGY P. 201 MIDDLE, TOP

Bob Swanson/Swanson Image
CENTRAL PLAZA 1,3

Douglas Symes
WASHINGTON/MONTGOMERY 1-6
CHRONOLOGY P. 201 LEFT, BOTTOM

D. Tomlinson
CHRONOLOGY P. 200 RIGHT, MIDDLE

Alan Weintraub
HI-DESERT MEDICAL CENTER

All other images courtesy KMD